The Story of Inventions

The Story of Inventions

Anna Claybourne

Illustrated by Adam Larkum

Designed by Steve Wood

Edited by Jane Chisholm

Additional designs by Stephen Wright

Cover design by Tom Lalonde

CONTENTS

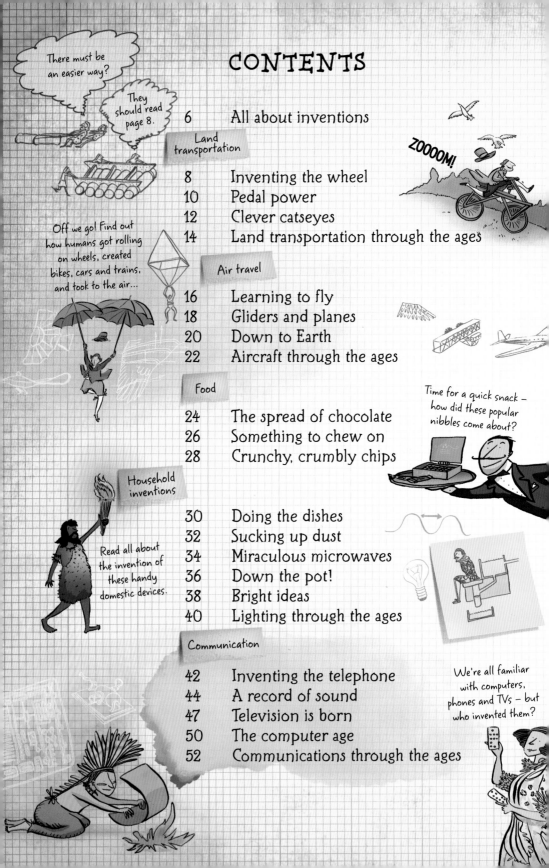

There must be an easier way?

They should read page 8.

Off we go! Find out how humans got rolling on wheels, created bikes, cars and trains, and took to the air...

ZOOOOM!

Time for a quick snack — how did these popular nibbles come about?

Read all about the invention of these handy domestic devices.

We're all familiar with computers, phones and TVs — but who invented them?

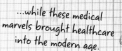

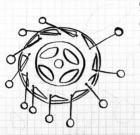

ALL ABOUT INVENTIONS

Humans have always been inventors. Since prehistoric times, we've been using the materials around us to create useful tools, gadgets and toys. And we're not showing any signs of stopping.

Why invent?

Many inventions help us to do jobs more quickly and easily – the dishwasher, for example. Others, like the catseye, make life safer. And some, such as photography, let us do things we couldn't do before. Invention is the key to progress. It's given us the modern world we have today.

Ouch! That's sharp!

Makes a great knife though.

Even animals invent things!

Humans aren't the only inventors. Intelligent animals such as chimpanzees have invented many kinds of tools. Some use rocks to crack open nuts, and some strip the leaves off twigs, then use the twigs to pull termites out of their nests to eat.

Many minds

Some inventions are the work of just one person. For example, Percy Shaw came up with the idea for the catseye in a flash, after he was inspired by seeing a cat on the road at night. Most inventions, though, develop over a long time, with lots of different inventors adding their own ideas.

Get a patent!

As you'll find out in this book, inventors often rush to patent their inventions as soon as they can. A patent is a kind of government license for an invention.

Patent pictures

To apply for a patent, you have to send in a description of your invention, along with clear drawings showing what it is and how it works. These pictures are based on patent drawings for two famous inventions:

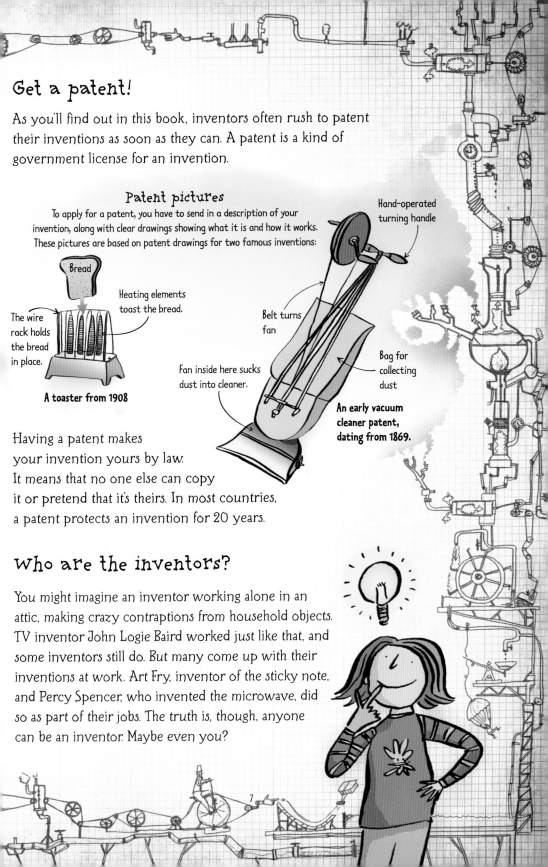

Bread

The wire rack holds the bread in place.

Heating elements toast the bread.

A toaster from 1908

Hand-operated turning handle

Belt turns fan

Bag for collecting dust

Fan inside here sucks dust into cleaner.

An early vacuum cleaner patent, dating from 1869.

Having a patent makes your invention yours by law. It means that no one else can copy it or pretend that it's theirs. In most countries, a patent protects an invention for 20 years.

Who are the inventors?

You might imagine an inventor working alone in an attic, making crazy contraptions from household objects. TV inventor John Logie Baird worked just like that, and some inventors still do. But many come up with their inventions at work. Art Fry, inventor of the sticky note, and Percy Spencer, who invented the microwave, did so as part of their jobs. The truth is, though, anyone can be an inventor. Maybe even you?

Inventing the wheel

I magine life without wheels. With no cars, trains, bikes or buses – or even wheelbarrows – getting around would be miserably slow. Luckily, wheels were invented a long, long time ago.

Wheel-free world

6,000 years ago, no one had wheels. But it didn't matter so much, as in those days, there were hardly any roads. Many people lived in forests, deserts or boggy swamps, where wheels wouldn't have been much use. They walked everywhere, and used animals to carry heavy loads.

Nobody knows exactly where or when the first wheel was invented, but the earliest pictures of wheels are around 5,200 years old, and come from Sumeria (an ancient civilization in what is now Iraq). They show carts with solid wooden wheels made from planks, pulled by onagers (a type of wild donkey). It would have been a bumpy ride, but wheels helped the Sumerians to travel faster and carry loads much more easily than before.

No wheels please, we're Incas!
Early people in the Americas, such as the Incas, never had wheels. They did without. They didn't see wheels until the 1400s, when explorers from Europe came to America, bringing wheeled carts and cannons with them.

The Incas used llamas to carry heavy loads.

Potters' wheels?
A few experts think that wheels were actually first invented by Sumerian potters to spin clay pots on. Other people may then have copied the potters' wheels and used them to make vehicles.

Early Sumerian cart

Onagers pulled the cart.

Wheels were made of two planks fixed together and cut into a circle shape.

Wheels of progress

Most experts think wheels developed slowly over many, many years.
They probably weren't invented by a single person.

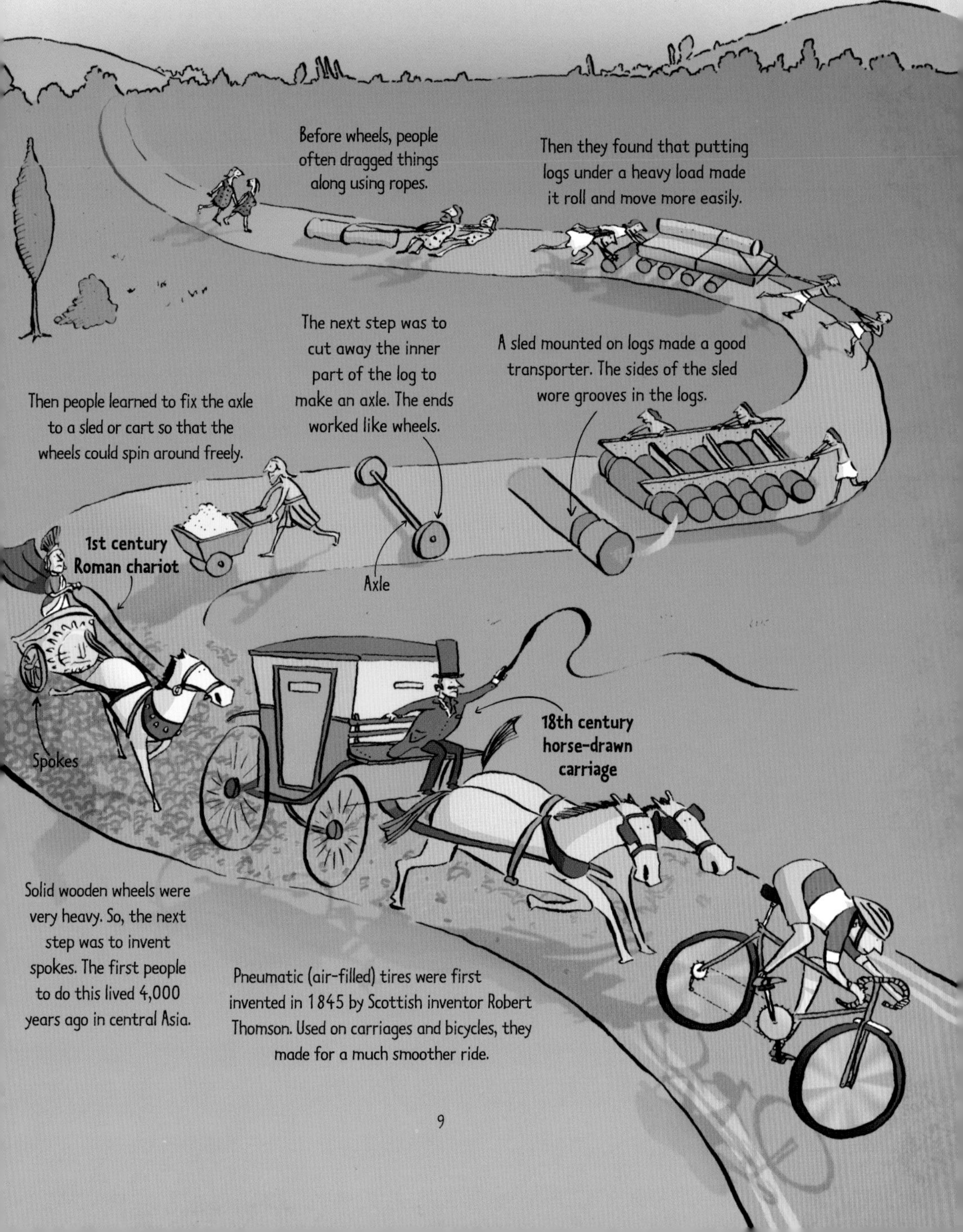

Before wheels, people often dragged things along using ropes.

Then they found that putting logs under a heavy load made it roll and move more easily.

The next step was to cut away the inner part of the log to make an axle. The ends worked like wheels.

A sled mounted on logs made a good transporter. The sides of the sled wore grooves in the logs.

Then people learned to fix the axle to a sled or cart so that the wheels could spin around freely.

1st century Roman chariot

Axle

18th century horse-drawn carriage

Spokes

Solid wooden wheels were very heavy. So, the next step was to invent spokes. The first people to do this lived 4,000 years ago in central Asia.

Pneumatic (air-filled) tires were first invented in 1845 by Scottish inventor Robert Thomson. Used on carriages and bicycles, they made for a much smoother ride.

9

Pedal power

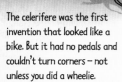

T he bicycle is a simple invention that needs no engine, electronics or fuel. It's so simple, it could have been invented a thousand years ago – but in fact, it only came along quite recently.

The celerifere was the first invention that looked like a bike. But it had no pedals and couldn't turn corners – not unless you did a wheelie.

Rolling along

In about 1790, Frenchman Mede de Sivrac invented something called a "celerifere." It was made of wood and had two wheels, but no pedals or steering. It soon became fashionable to whizz downhill on one.

But German baron Karl von Drais saw room for improvement. In 1817, he designed a version of the celerifere, but with a front wheel that could be steered, using handlebars. Riding a "Draisienne" bike became a popular sport in many parts of Europe.

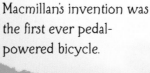

Steerable handlebars made the Draisienne much easier to use.

Pedals at last!

As these early bikes had no pedals, you had to push them along the ground with your feet. But in 1839, Scottish blacksmith Kirkpatrick Macmillan built a new metal model, with foot levers that turned the back wheel. Locals who saw him zooming around on his machine laughed at him – especially when he crashed into a child and was fined. But Macmillan's invention was the first ever pedal-powered bicycle.

Macmillan's bicycle used pedal power to push the bike along. It allowed him to ride a long way without getting tired out.

10

Front-wheel drive

Macmillan never patented or manufactured his design. Instead, other people copied it and came up with their own variations. Paris carriage-makers Ernest and Pierre Michaux launched their version in the 1850s. It had pedals attached to a large front wheel, and was called the "velocipede" – French for "fast-foot."

Velocipedes had solid rubber tires and were very uncomfortable. In England they were called "boneshakers."

High and hazardous

The bigger the front wheel, the faster a velocipede could go. In 1871, English inventor James Starley designed one with a huge front wheel. He named it the "Ordinary," though it looks very strange now. It went fast, but was very wobbly and caused lots of accidents.

The Ordinary was later nicknamed the "penny farthing" after two English coins.

Safe AND fast

James Starley's nephew John Starley solved the problem in 1885. He linked the pedals to a chain that turned the back wheel, as on Macmillan's bike. Both wheels were the same size, and the bike was so much safer it was named the "safety bicycle." Bikes today still work in the same way.

Leonardo's bike?

In the 1960s, monks found a drawing dating from 1493 in a notebook belonging to the Italian artist and inventor Leonardo da Vinci. It showed a contraption uncannily like a modern bike. Had he invented the bicycle 400 years ahead of time? No one knows. Many people today think the sketch might be a fake.

Modern bike

Safety bike

Clever catseyes

A single, brillant idea made Percy Shaw one of the most successful inventors ever. He wasn't an engineer or a scientist, but he had a brainwave that led to a great invention, and it made him a millionaire.

Night Fright

Percy Shaw was born in Halifax, England in 1890. As a boy he loved inventing his own games and tools, and when he grew up he built his own roller for smoothing roads. With it he went into business as a road mender.

One dark, foggy night in 1933, driving home from Bradford to Halifax, Shaw nearly drove off the road and over a cliff. He was saved because he saw two small bright lights by the roadside – the eyes of a stray cat, reflecting his car headlights.

This gave Shaw an idea for a reflector to mark the sides of the road at night, which would work just like a cat's eye. After trying various designs, he came up with this:

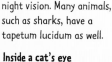

Meow!

Real cats' eyes

Why do real cats' eyes reflect light? It's because they have a silvery layer at the back, called the "tapetum lucidum" (Latin for "bright carpet"). It makes light pass through the cat's retina (the light-sensitive part of the eye) twice, giving cats better night vision. Many animals, such as sharks, have a tapetum lucidum as well.

Inside a cat's eye

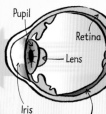

Light

Pupil

Retina

Lens

Iris

Tapetum lucidum

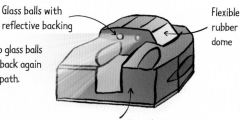

Glass balls with reflective backing

Flexible rubber dome

Light shines into glass balls and is reflected back again along the same path.

Cast iron base or "shoe" which can be attached to road surface

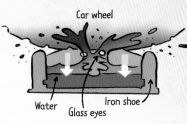

Car wheel

Water   Glass eyes   Iron shoe

When it rains, water collects in the iron shoe. Whenever a car drives over the catseye, it squashes down the dome containing the glass eyes. They are pushed into the rainwater and washed clean.

Self-cleaning catseyes

Shaw's invention – now known as the "catseye" – not only lit up the road at night with no electricity; it could also clean itself with rainwater. This picture shows how:

Lighting the world's roads

Shaw patented his invention in 1934, and set up his own factory. As a test, he put 50 catseyes along a dangerous local road. The accident rate plummeted.

In 1937, the British government ran a competition to find the best road reflector, and Shaw's catseye won it. Within a few years, his factory was making catseyes for use across Britain, and for roads all over the world. Catseyes have probably saved thousands of lives.

Staying at home
Though the catseye made Percy Shaw rich, he didn't let success go to his head. He stayed in Halifax, in the house where he had grown up, until his death at the age of 86. He spent his money on two Rolls Royce cars and on throwing parties for his friends, but refused to buy any carpets or curtains.

New directions

Today, there are more cars and roads than ever, and catseyes are still in use. Many roads now have catseyes along the middle as well as at the edges. And catseyes are no longer just white – red ones are often used at the edges of big roads, and green ones are used at junctions. There are even solar-powered catseyes that give off their own light. But they are still made to Percy Shaw's basic design.

Vrooom!

LAND TRANSPORTATION
THROUGH THE AGES

For thousands of years, land vehicles were powered by horses - or humans. People could hardly imagine a carriage that went by itself...

People make millions of journeys every day – mostly on land. And we've invented loads of ways to get from A to B.

... but that became possible with the invention of steam engines by Denis Papin, in 1690.

1690 — The steam engine

A steam engine turns the pushing power of steam into movement.

2. As the piston moves up and down, it pushes a lever, making it move.

3. The lever can be used to power a machine.

Piston

1. Steam from boiling water pushes the piston up. It drops back down as the steam cools.

Boiling water

Fire

1769 — Steam-powered wagon

In 1769, French inventor Nicholas-Joseph Cugnot built a wagon powered by a steam engine. It was probably the first ever steam-powered vehicle.

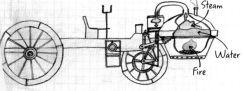

Steam

Water

Fire

But Cugnot's steam wagon was slow and hard to drive. In 1771 it crashed into a brick wall.

1804 — Steam trains

Inventors soon realized steam engines worked better with trains than with wagons. British inventor Richard Trevithick built the first steam train in 1804. By the 1830s, trains such as the Rocket, built by George Stephenson, were carrying paying passengers.

Stephenson's Rocket could go at 50km/h (30mph). Some people were afraid that travel at this huge speed might be bad for you.

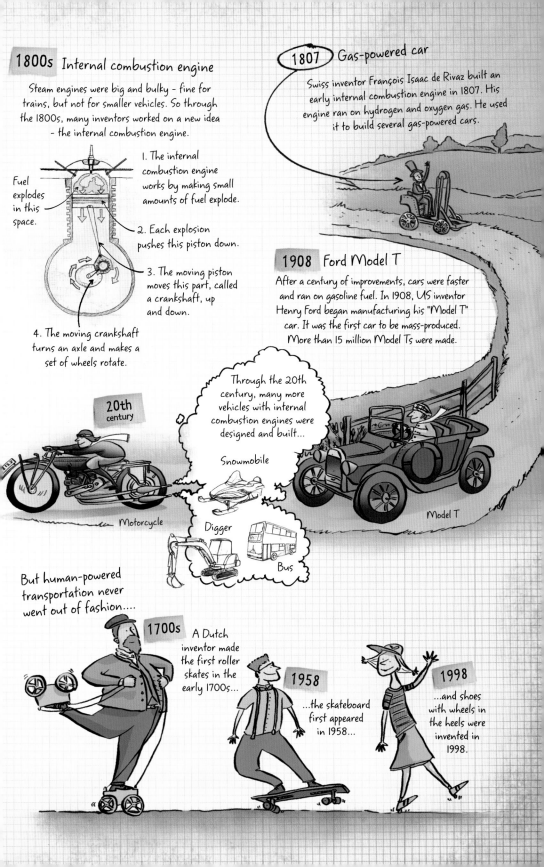

1800s Internal combustion engine

Steam engines were big and bulky - fine for trains, but not for smaller vehicles. So through the 1800s, many inventors worked on a new idea - the internal combustion engine.

Fuel explodes in this space.

1. The internal combustion engine works by making small amounts of fuel explode.

2. Each explosion pushes this piston down.

3. The moving piston moves this part, called a crankshaft, up and down.

4. The moving crankshaft turns an axle and makes a set of wheels rotate.

1807 Gas-powered car

Swiss inventor François Isaac de Rivaz built an early internal combustion engine in 1807. His engine ran on hydrogen and oxygen gas. He used it to build several gas-powered cars.

1908 Ford Model T

After a century of improvements, cars were faster and ran on gasoline fuel. In 1908, US inventor Henry Ford began manufacturing his "Model T" car. It was the first car to be mass-produced. More than 15 million Model Ts were made.

20th century

Through the 20th century, many more vehicles with internal combustion engines were designed and built...

Snowmobile

Motorcycle

Digger

Bus

Model T

But human-powered transportation never went out of fashion....

1700s A Dutch inventor made the first roller skates in the early 1700s...

1958 ...the skateboard first appeared in 1958...

1998 ...and shoes with wheels in the heels were invented in 1998.

Learning to fly

Humans have always watched birds, bats and insects flying around, and wanted to fly too. But early flying experiments took a while to get off the ground...

Fly like a bird

Birds fly by flapping their wings, so why can't we? It's all because of the shape and design of a bird's body. Unlike us, birds are built for flying...

Huge chest muscles provide enough power for flapping.

Tiny legs reduce body weight.

Hollow bones make birds' bodies light.

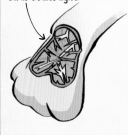

In a flap

For their first attempts at flying, people copied birds. They built big feathered wings, strapped them to their arms, and started flapping.

Scottish scientist John Damian tried this in 1507. Wearing wings made from chicken feathers, he leaped off Stirling Castle in Scotland, planning to fly to France. Instead, he fell straight into a dungheap and broke his leg.

Aaarrrgghh!

Damian thought he should have used eagle feathers instead of chicken feathers. But he was wrong. Inventors have tried all kinds of different designs – and feathers – but no amount of flapping can keep a human in the air.

A flying machine with flapping wings is called an ornithopter.

It'll never fly.

Ornithopter with wheels attached

Lighter than air

Hot air is lighter than cold air, which means it can float above it. The ancient Chinese knew this. They invented hot-air-filled flying lanterns that floated into the sky.

How it works

If you heat air, its molecules spread out and it gets lighter.

The hot air inside the lantern is lighter than the cooler air around it.

The cool, heavy air sinks and the warm air floats up, pulling the lantern with it.

Balloon brainwave

In 1783, two French brothers named Joseph and Jacques Montgolfier decided to use this idea to make a much bigger, passenger-carrying hot-air flying machine.

The brothers belonged to a paper-making family, so they had plenty of paper. In 1783, they made a huge balloon out of paper and cloth, and filled it with hot air from a fire.

Up, up and away!

The brothers' first balloon flew nearly 2km (1.2 miles) by itself. Their next test flight carried a duck, a rooster and a sheep into the sky.

Finally, the Montgolfiers built a hot-air balloon that could carry people. Two brave volunteers, a science teacher and a soldier, made the first human flight on November 21 1783, floating for 8km (5 miles) over the streets of Paris.

Gulp!

The balloon was filled with hot air, heated by a huge fire on the ground.

Gliders and planes

Humans first flew in hot-air balloons in 1783. But balloons were slow and hard to steer. Inventors still wanted to copy birds, and fly fast and far on a pair of wings.

Gliding wings

Birds like this eagle glide with their wings spread out. The position and shape of the wings lift the bird as it moves forward.

Gliding along...

Flapping wings had proved useless. But 19th century inventor George Cayley saw that the wings didn't have to flap. Instead, they could stick straight out, like the wings of a gliding eagle. He made a series of bird-like flying models, with curved, tilted wings and a streamlined shape.

Finally, in 1849, Cayley built a working glider, and tested it with a 10-year old boy on board. When pulled downhill, it took off and flew a short way. In 1853, Cayley built a new glider and persuaded his coachman, John Appleby, to pilot it. It flew for 183m (610ft). Appleby was terrified and complained, "I was hired to drive, not fly!"

Cayley copied this streamlined shape from the body of a trout. He saw that it would be a good shape for a glider's body.

He tried out various wing shapes and designs...

...and finally designed whole, working gliders.

Cayley's 1853 glider

Yikes!

John Appleby

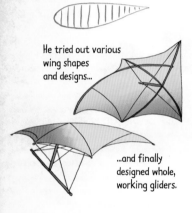

...on the wings of a bird

German engineer Otto Lilienthal was the next great glider inventor. To achieve the perfect shape, he studied birds' wings and tails. He built 18 gliders and flew them all himself, making hundreds of flights in the 1890s. Sadly, he died in a glider crash in 1896. But his brilliant glider designs paved the way for future inventors.

Lilienthal's gliders were based on his sketches of birds.

18

Powered flight

Gliders could only fly a short way, because they had no power to push them through the air. The answer was to add a propeller, powered by an engine. But the first inventors to try this didn't have much luck, because the engines that were available were too heavy.

In 1890, Clement Ader managed a very short flight in his propeller-driven "Ader Eole" – but couldn't keep it going.

Getting it Wright

American brothers Orville and Wilbur Wright wanted to build a powered glider too. As they couldn't find an engine light enough, they designed and built their own to fit onto their plane, the "Wright Flyer."

The Flyer's first powered test run, on December 14 1903, went wrong when the plane tilted and stalled soon after leaving the ground. But three days later, on December 17, with Orville Wright on board, the Wright Flyer flew for 12 seconds, covering 37m (120ft). It was the first sustained, powered flight in history.

The Wright brothers began with a simple, unmanned, kite-like glider in 1900, before developing their plane.

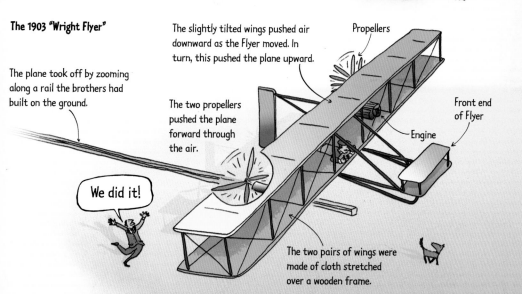

The 1903 "Wright Flyer"

The slightly tilted wings pushed air downward as the Flyer moved. In turn, this pushed the plane upward.

Propellers

The plane took off by zooming along a rail the brothers had built on the ground.

The two propellers pushed the plane forward through the air.

Engine

Front end of Flyer

We did it!

The two pairs of wings were made of cloth stretched over a wooden frame.

Down to Earth

Parachutes were invented long before planes. The ancient Chinese and Leonardo da Vinci (see left) both designed early versions. But the first known actual parachute jumps happened around 400 years ago.

who jumped first?

The first parachutist to win fame was Louis-Sebastien Lenormand of France. In 1783 he jumped from a tree, then from a tower, holding two parasols. Their umbrella-shape trapped air beneath them, which slowed his fall. Inspired by his parasols, Lenormand came up with the name "parachute." "Parasol" means "against the sun" and "parachute" means "against a fall."

However, the first true parachute jump had actually taken place over 150 years earlier. In 1617, a little-known Croatian inventor, Faust Vrancic, tried out a device he called a "fall breaker," jumping safely from a tower in Venice.

Leonardo's chute

In about 1485, Italian inventor Leonardo da Vinci sketched a design for a simple parachute.

Leonardo's design was a square cone with a fixed frame.

In the year 2000, skydivers built and tested a version of Leonardo's chute. It worked!

Vrancic's "fall-breaker" was a curved, rectangular canopy, similar in shape to some modern parachutes.

Lenormand used two large parasols as a parachute. He jumped first from a small tree, then from a high tower in Paris, without injury.

Wheee!

Most early
parachutes were
cone- or umbrella-
shaped, made of canvas
fixed to a wooden frame.

I can do that!

Through the 1780s, inspired by Lenormand's jumps, several other French inventors and stunt performers began parachuting. They experimented with new parachute designs – and with much higher jumps.

In 1785, balloonist Jean Pierre Blanchard showed how a parachute could be used to escape from a hot-air balloon and descend safely to the ground. At first, he used a dog to demonstrate the device, but later he tried it out himself.

Soon after that, in 1797, stuntman André Jacques Garnerin made a thrilling parachute jump from a balloon 1,000m (3,218ft) up in the air.

Folding flat

Early parachutes were rigid, with a wooden frame to hold them open. In around 1795, inventors developed folding parachutes with collapsing frames, then soft silk parachutes with no frame at all. These could be folded up into a backpack, then opened using a ripcord. This made it easier to carry and store parachutes when they weren't in use.

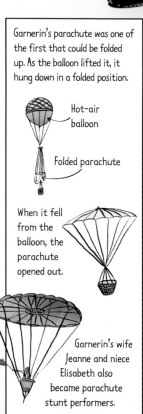

Garnerin's parachute was one of the first that could be folded up. As the balloon lifted it, it hung down in a folded position.

Hot-air
balloon

Folded parachute

When it fell
from the
balloon, the
parachute
opened out.

Garnerin's wife
Jeanne and niece
Elisabeth also
became parachute
stunt performers.

Planes and parachutes

The first planes flew in 1903, and in 1911 the first parachute jumps were made from moving planes. In the 20th century, parachutes became essential equipment for the armed forces, for dropping soldiers into war zones and allowing pilots to escape from damaged aircraft. Today, people also go parachuting and skydiving just for fun.

Skydivers freefall through
the air before opening
their parachutes.

Giffard's airship was filled with hydrogen gas to give it lift.

AIRCRAFT
THROUGH THE AGES

Ever since hot-air balloons and planes were invented, people have been finding all kinds of new ways and new reasons to take to the air.

1852 Airship — It was driven forward by a steam engine.

French inventor Henri Giffard built and flew the first airship in 1852.

Spy balloon 1860s

Balloons were great for spying on enemy troops from above.

Early hot-air balloons were used for viewing the battlefield in the American Civil War in the 1860s.

WASHINGT

early 1900s Biplane

The first powered planes were built by the Wright brothers. They were biplanes with two sets of wings.

One of the Wright brothers' biplanes

1905 Monoplane

The 1909 Blériot monoplane XI

Then, people started making planes with just one pair of wings. They called them monoplanes.

1914 Airliner

This Benoist Model 14 flying boat was used by the first ever airline. It carried passengers between St. Petersburg and Tampa, two cities in Florida.

1914-18 Fighter plane

Before long, planes were being used in warfare. This is a Fokker DR.I, a military plane used by the Germans in the First World War (1914-18).

1930s Jet plane

Jet engines were developed in the 1930s. The first jet plane, the Heinkel HE178, took to the air in 1939.

Jet engine

Combustion chamber

Exhaust

Air intake

Compressor

Fuel injector

Turbine

The exhaust shooting out of the back of a jet engine creates a strong forward-pushing force.

1936 Helicopter

In 1936, German professor Heinrich Focke built the first practical helicopter, the twin-rotor Model 61.

Since then, helicopters have been used in warfare, crime-fighting, sightseeing and rescues.

1940s Jet airliner

The first jet airliner was the Comet, launched in 1949. It could carry about 36 passengers.

Many people dream of flying by jetpack, a personal flying machine often seen in sci-fi films. Real jetpacks were first flown in the 1940s – but, so far, they are not cheap or practical enough for us all to have one.

In the 1950s, air travel became widespread, and passenger planes gradually grew bigger and bigger.

1977 Pedal-powered plane

The Gossamer Condor was the first pedal-powered plane.

Large horizontal stabilizer

The pilot had to pedal fast to power the propeller.

The lightweight carbon-fiber frame was wrapped in clear plastic.

2007 Full-length double-decker

In 2007, plane company Airbus launched the biggest passenger plane ever built, the double-decker Airbus A380.

The A380 can carry up to 555 passengers.

There's even space for on-board bars and shops.

Seating

Cabins

Elevator

Seating

Restaurant

Duty-free shop

Bar

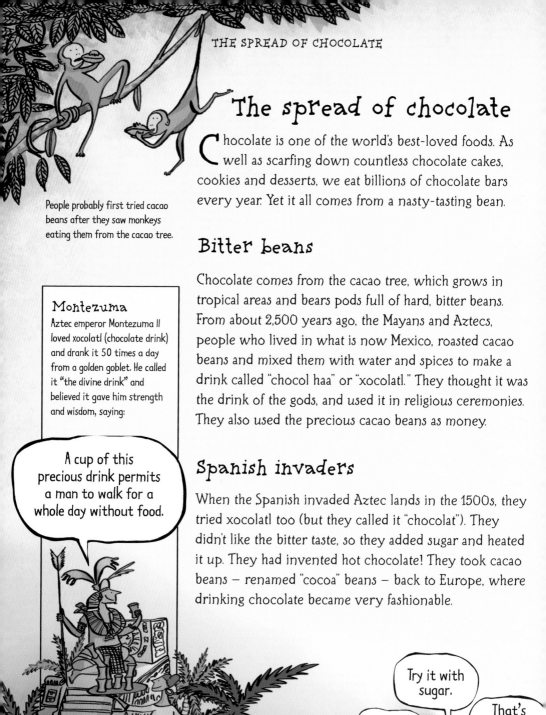

The spread of chocolate

Chocolate is one of the world's best-loved foods. As well as scarfing down countless chocolate cakes, cookies and desserts, we eat billions of chocolate bars every year. Yet it all comes from a nasty-tasting bean.

People probably first tried cacao beans after they saw monkeys eating them from the cacao tree.

Bitter beans

Chocolate comes from the cacao tree, which grows in tropical areas and bears pods full of hard, bitter beans. From about 2,500 years ago, the Mayans and Aztecs, people who lived in what is now Mexico, roasted cacao beans and mixed them with water and spices to make a drink called "chocol haa" or "xocolatl." They thought it was the drink of the gods, and used it in religious ceremonies. They also used the precious cacao beans as money.

Montezuma
Aztec emperor Montezuma II loved xocolatl (chocolate drink) and drank it 50 times a day from a golden goblet. He called it "the divine drink" and believed it gave him strength and wisdom, saying:

A cup of this precious drink permits a man to walk for a whole day without food.

Spanish invaders

When the Spanish invaded Aztec lands in the 1500s, they tried xocolatl too (but they called it "chocolat"). They didn't like the bitter taste, so they added sugar and heated it up. They had invented hot chocolate! They took cacao beans – renamed "cocoa" beans – back to Europe, where drinking chocolate became very fashionable.

Try it with sugar.

Bleurgh...

That's better!

Chocolate bars

By the 1700s, special chocolate cafés had sprung up across Europe. Chocolate was very expensive, though, so only the rich and famous could afford it.

For centuries, Europeans had their chocolate as a drink, just like the Mayans and Aztecs. Some bakers used it in cakes, but there was no such thing as a chocolate bar.

In 1847, Francis Fry, who belonged to a famous family of chocolate-sellers, decided to make solid chocolate — chocolate you could eat! He heated smooth cocoa powder and fatty cocoa butter — both extracted from cocoa beans — and stirred in some sugar. When the mixture cooled, it hardened into chocolate bars.

Chocolate explosion

The first chocolate bars were a bit chewy and gritty, but chocolatiers (chocolate-makers) kept experimenting to create better and better chocolate.

• In 1853 the Fry family launched the chocolate cream, the first chocolate-coated candy bar.
• Milk chocolate was invented in 1879.
• In 1912, Jean Neuhaus developed the hard chocolate shell, making chocolates with soft fillings possible.

New chocolate creations are still being invented today, and people are eating more chocolate than ever before.

Chocolate ships

The Spanish grew cocoa beans on plantations in Africa and shipped them to Spain. In 1579, pirates raided a Spanish ship, thinking it was carrying gold. Instead, it was full of cocoa beans. The pirates thought they were sheep droppings, so they set fire to them! If they had known the truth, they could have sold the beans for a fortune.

Fry found a way to blend cocoa butter with cocoa powder to make a paste.

He dissolved sugar into the warm mixture to sweeten it.

Then he poured the chocolate into molds to cool and harden.

Francis Fry designed the mold for the Fry's Chocolate Cream. It is still the same shape today.

Something to chew on

The ancient Greeks chewed mastiche, the resin of the mastic tree...

P eople have been chewing rubbery tree sap since prehistory. The chewing gum we know today, though, dates from 1869, thanks to a meeting between a Mexican rebel leader and a US inventor.

Humans have a natural urge to chew. That's why we chew pencils and fingernails. And since ancient times, people have looked for chewy stuff to pop in their mouths, such as a kind of tree sap called chicle.

...and the Mayans of Mexico chewed chicle, the sap of the sapodilla tree.

A man with a plan

In the 1800s in America, you could buy spruce gum or paraffin wax for chewing. But it wasn't very nice. It was hard, crumbly and tasted bad.

All that changed when Antonio Lopez de Santa Anna, a Mexican rebel leader and dictator, was thrown out of Mexico after he lost power. He came to stay with an inventor friend, Thomas Adams, in New York City in 1869.

Santa Anna may have lost his job as a politician, but he had a plan to make some money. He brought a load of chewy chicle from Mexico, hoping that his inventor friend could use it in place of rubber to invent a new kind of tire.

Adams tried making tires, toys and rain boots with the chicle, but they all failed. Chicle couldn't be worked in the same way as rubber. The process used to turn it into useful shapes made it too hard. It seemed that the chicle was useless.

Sap and resin

Sap and resin are natural substances from trees. Resin is a sticky gum that some trees make to seal up cuts. Sap is liquid that flows through a tree, a bit like blood. Some saps can be boiled to make a gum.

Like chicle, rubber is made from sap collected from trees.

26

A new idea

In his frustration, Adams decided to throw all the chicle into the local river. But before he did, he stopped at a local store, and saw a girl buying some paraffin wax gum.

Adams suddenly had a brainwave. The chicle — which the Mexicans had chewed for centuries — would make great chewing gum.

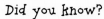

Before chicle became widespread, chewing gum tasted horrible and soon crumbled to bits.

Production line

Adams and his son Tom set to work. They made the chicle into chewing gum lozenges, wrapped them in bright tissue paper, and took them to local candy stores. They were so popular, they sold out in days.

Adams soon patented a gum-making machine and opened a chewing gum factory. Before long, he started selling gum from vending machines too. The chicle gum was a huge hit, because it was smoother, softer and more chewy than other gums. Flavors could be added too, such as peppermint and tutti frutti.

A package of Adams New York No. 1 brand chewing gum — one of Thomas Adams's first products. It used the slogan "snapping and stretching."

Gum goes global

Today, gum is chewed around the world. There's bubblegum too — extra-stretchy gum invented in 1928 by Walter Diemer. In fact, so many people chew gum now that we've had to invent new machines that can clean all the chewed, gooey mess off the streets!

Did you know?
A US dentist, William Finlay Semple, invented another type of chewing gum at the same time as Adams. He designed it to keep teeth clean and exercise the jaw. But it was made of rock-hard rubber, and was not a huge sucess.

I demand THIN French fries!

Crunchy, crumbly chips!

Chips were invented by the aptly named George Crum. A chef at a fancy restaurant, Crum came up with chips thanks to a grumpy customer's complaint.

"Fix these French fries!"

In the 1850s, the Moon Lake Lodge in Saratoga Springs, New York, was a top luxury eating spot for rich customers. One of them was Cornelius Vanderbilt, a famous railroad millionaire. During a visit to the restaurant in 1853, Vanderbilt ordered some French fries – but when they came, he hated them. He sent them back to the kitchen, moaning that they were far too thick and chewy. He wanted his fries thinner and crispier.

Why ARE chips so delicious?

In prehistoric times, humans needed to store body fat for the winter. So we are programmed to love and crave fatty foods.

Chips are made by slicing potatoes thinly before frying them. Lots of thin slices means lots of surface area to soak up lots of fat. The result is a crispy, fat-filled snack that most people love. Sadly, there's so much fat in them that chips aren't very good for you.

"Certainly, sir!"

In the kitchen, the chef, George Crum, made some thinner, crispier fries especially for Vanderbilt. But Vanderbilt sent them back again, saying they *still* weren't thin enough!

This time, Crum was really annoyed. To teach the fusspot a lesson, he sliced some potatoes as thinly as he could, fried them for far too long until they were brown and crispy, and threw salt all over them.

You can guess the rest. Vanderbilt loved the crispy, crumbly fries and ordered more. Word of Crum's creation spread fast. Soon, his ultra-thin fries were the restaurant's signature dish.

Yum... delicious...

Chips with everything

At first Crum's chips, known as "Saratoga chips," were served as part of a main course. When Crum started his own restaurant, he always put a free basket of chips on the table, and people started eating them as a snack. Eventually, they were made in factories and sold in handy tins or tubs. They'd become a snack that anyone could eat, anytime.

Chips in a bag

The chip bag was invented by chip factory owner Laura Scudder in 1926. She noticed that chips in a tin or tub often went stale, so she began making bags out of wax paper, sealed with a hot iron. Chip bags today are still made in the same basic design, although they're now made of plastic instead of paper.

Laura Scudder

Tasty Taytos

At first, chips were plain, and came with with a tiny bag of salt to pour onto them. Flavored chips didn't come along until 1954, when Joe Murphy, owner of the Tayto® crisp factory in Ireland, began making them.

The first flavors Murphy made were salt and vinegar and cheese and onion – which are still popular today. Murphy's idea revolutionized the world of chips, and today, flavored chips are the norm. You can buy hundreds of different varieties – from chili, roast chicken, baked bean and sausage, to cheese and chive and tomato ketchup.

It's a date!

As well as chip bags, Laura Scudder invented use-by dates. She was the first manufacturer to put dates on her products as they left the factory, so people could check that they were fresh.

Salt'n'Shake chips

29

We won't wash ourselves, you know!

Doing the dishes

Few inventions can be more loved than the dishwasher, which saves you from doing the dishes. Women have done most of the dishwashing – so not surprisingly it was a woman who invented this dirtbusting device.

Dirty dish dilemma

Josephine Garis Cochran was a wealthy society lady living in Illinois, in the early 1880s. As a rich woman with plenty of servants, she didn't have to wash her own dirty dishes at all. But she did, because she was tired of her servants being careless and chipping her valuable plates and cups.

But Josephine still hated washing the dishes as much as anyone. It took hours and made her hands wrinkled, and she wished there was a machine to do it for her. Eventually she declared:

Early attempt

Several people had already tried to invent a dishwasher. One was US inventor Joel Houghton, who patented the first ever dishwasher design in 1850, over 30 years before Cochran. Houghton's dishwasher was made of wood and had a hand-cranked wheel that splashed the dishes with water. The trouble was, it didn't get them clean...

If nobody else is going to invent a dishwashing machine, I'll do it myself!

Setting to work

Josephine had learned about engineering from her father, John Garis, a famous builder, and her grandfather, John Fitch, an inventor. So she set up a workshop in her backyard, and started inventing. When her husband died in 1883, making her less wealthy, she worked even harder. Finally, she perfected a brilliant dishwasher design...

30

How it worked

Josephine Cochran's dishwasher worked by squirting hot soapy water, heated in a boiler, at the dishes. Then it rinsed them with clean water. The dishes were held in a wire rack.

Cochran's small hand-powered dishwasher for use in the home

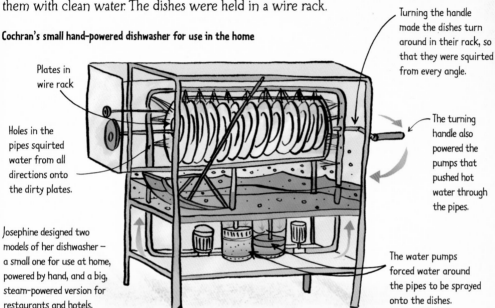

Turning the handle made the dishes turn around in their rack, so that they were squirted from every angle.

Plates in wire rack

Holes in the pipes squirted water from all directions onto the dirty plates.

Josephine designed two models of her dishwasher – a small one for use at home, powered by hand, and a big, steam-powered version for restaurants and hotels.

The turning handle also powered the pumps that pushed hot water through the pipes.

The water pumps forced water around the pipes to be sprayed onto the dishes.

A new career

Josephine patented her invention in 1886, and showed it at the 1893 Chicago World's Fair (a huge science and culture exhibition) where it won an award. She set up a business to make dishwashers, and sold them to lots of hotels and restaurants. Her company, Cochran's Crescent Washing Machine Company, eventually became the KitchenAid® company, which still exists.

Because they were expensive, dishwashers didn't really catch on in the home until the 1950s, long after Josephine Cochran had died. Today, though, they're everywhere – and they still work in the same basic way as Cochran's design.

Did you know?

Many modern appliances use up a lot of energy, and are more wasteful than doing jobs by hand. But dishwashers are different. Using some modern dishwashers (as long as it's full, not half-empty) can use less hot water and energy than hand-washing your dishes.

A modern dishwasher

Cough, cough!

Simple twig brooms were invented more than 4,000 years ago.

Sucking up dust

Before vacuum cleaners, there were two ways to clean your carpet: sweeping it with a broom, or beating it with a stick. Both created clouds of choking dust.

Sucking it up

A vacuum cleaner uses a vacuum – an empty space – to create a sucking force that pulls in dust and dirt. This idea dates from 1860, when US inventor Daniel Hess designed a carpet sweeper with bellows on top that lifted up to create a vacuum. And in 1869, another American, Ives McGaffey, invented the hand-operated "Whirlwind" cleaner, which used a fan to suck in dust. Unfortunately, both these early versions failed to take off.

Hess's suction sweeper

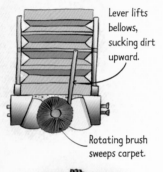

Lever lifts bellows, sucking dirt upward.

Rotating brush sweeps carpet.

Booth's big breakthrough

English engineer Hubert Cecil Booth is often considered to be the true inventor of the vacuum cleaner. His oil-powered cleaner, invented in 1901, used a motor pump to create suction. It was so huge it had to be pulled from house to house on a horse-drawn cart. Assistants then put long tubes through the windows and used them to suck the dirt out of the house.

Party time!

Booth's vacuum cleaner was popular with the rich and was even used by royalty. By 1903, society ladies were having vacuuming parties. They would invite their friends over to watch while workers used Booth's machine in their homes.

Hand-held hoovers

Booth's vacuum cleaner was such a success that other companies soon began to make them too. Several inventors came up with smaller vacuum cleaner designs, but it was an American caretaker, James Spangler, who finally got it right. He was so sick of dust making him cough when he did the cleaning that in 1907 he built his own dust-sucking machine. It was made from an electric fan, a wooden crate, a broomstick and a pillowcase.

Spangler sold his design to his cousin's husband, William Hoover, and he and Spangler went into business making vacuum cleaners. The simple, lightweight design made them a huge hit, and the Hoover® company sold millions of them. In some countries, domestic vacuum cleaners eventually became known as "hoovers."

Spangler's first design was very simple, but it still worked well.

Handle held bag and allowed the user to move the cleaner around.

Bag stored dust.

Fan sucked up dust into box.

One of the first Hoovers to go on sale, the Model 0

Still inventing

Though it was invented over a hundred years ago, the vacuum cleaner still isn't finished with. People keep inventing new ones.

In 1978, British inventor James Dyson invented the cyclone vacuum cleaner, which has no dust bag and uses a spinning cone to separate the dirt from the air. By the mid-1990s, cyclone cleaners outsold traditional dust-bag cleaners.

And in 2000, several companies brought out robot vacuum cleaners. They roam around a house by themselves, cleaning as they go.

Dust mites

What's in dust?

Vacuum cleaner salesmen often used to persuade people to buy a cleaner by telling them about the scary things in household dust. One teaspoon of dust can contain...

• 5 million skin cells
• 10,000 dust mites
• Hundreds of pet hairs
• Insect legs and eyes, and other creepy-crawly body parts
• Millions of bacteria and grains of plant pollen.

Miraculous microwaves

You put your popcorn, pizza or a nice big potato into the microwave oven, and after a few minutes – ding! it's done. Microwaves allow us to cook and heat food much faster than ever before.

What are microwaves?

Microwaves are a type of electromagnetic wave – like light waves, radio waves and x-rays. Electromagnetic waves have different wavelengths. For example, radio waves are long, and x-rays are very short. Microwaves, despite their name, are quite long.

Electromagnetic spectrum

Electromagnetic waves come in a range, or "spectrum," of wavelengths, as shown in this diagram.

The length of a wave is measured from one wave peak or "crest" to the next.

Wavelength

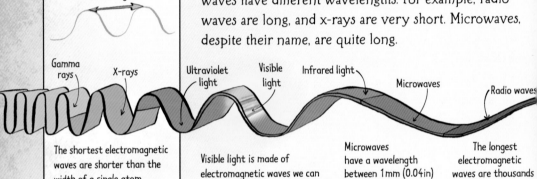

Gamma rays

X-rays

Ultraviolet light

Visible light

Infrared light

Microwaves

Radio waves

The shortest electromagnetic waves are shorter than the width of a single atom.

Visible light is made of electromagnetic waves we can see. We can't see microwaves.

Microwaves have a wavelength between 1mm (0.04in) and 30cm (12in).

The longest electromagnetic waves are thousands of miles long.

Radar works by bouncing microwaves off objects. It can be used to detect planes in flight.

Melting magnetron

During the Second World War, two British scientists, John Randall and Harry Boot, invented the magnetron, a device that emits microwaves, for use in radar equipment. An American company called Raytheon manufactured magnetrons. One day in 1945, a scientist at Raytheon, Percy Spencer, was working near a magnetron when he suddenly felt a strange warm sensation. A chocolate bar in his pocket had completely melted!

Aaaarrrggh!

Messy experiments

Percy wondered what could have created the heat that melted his chocolate. To find out, he decided to test the magnetron some more. He brought some unpopped popcorn into the lab. When he put it near the magnetron and switched it on, the popcorn popped.

Then he tried putting an egg into a metal pot, and aimed a beam of microwaves at it. It began to tremble as it heated up quickly inside. Just as one of Percy's colleagues peered closely at the egg... BANG! It exploded right in his face!

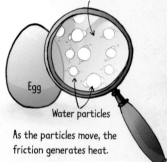

Microwave energy makes water particles in the egg vibrate.

Egg

Water particles

As the particles move, the friction generates heat.

Microwaves cook by making water particles in food vibrate. The vibrating particles rub together, and this rubbing, or friction, creates heat. Microwaves are not radioactive, unlike shorter electromagnetic waves such as gamma rays. So they don't harm people or do anything dangerous to the food.

Let's get cooking!

Percy Spencer soon designed a proper working microwave oven, and his company, Raytheon, started making it. The first model, the "1161 Radarange," was too big to use at home – it was nearly 2m (6ft) tall, and weighed as much as four men. But it was amazingly useful for hotels and restaurants.

In 1967, Raytheon launched small microwave ovens for the home. At first, many people were scared of the microwaves, thinking they might leak or be poisonous. But gradually they realized that no one was being harmed, and microwaves became popular. Now, almost every home has one.

Down the pot!

Roman public toilets

Seat

Water flowed along this channel into a drain.

The more people there are in the world, the more we need toilets to carry away our waste. Flushing toilets are an essential everyday invention. Imagine life without them...

Ancient toilets

The first simple flushing toilets date from thousands of years ago. The ancient Indian city of Harappa, and the Minoans of ancient Greece, both had indoor toilets 4,000 years ago. They were flushed into underground drains using jug of water or a flow of water from a stream. The Romans had public toilet blocks with rows of holes to sit over. Water flowed along a channel underneath to wash everything away.

500 years ago, a chamber pot like this would have been your toilet.

The royal toilet

Although ancient peoples had gone to the trouble of designing proper toilets, their inventions were gradually forgotten about. In the Middle Ages most people used a chamber pot, then emptied it into the street. Yuck!

Then, in 1596, Sir John Harington, a godson of Queen Elizabeth I of England, created the first modern flushing toilet. Sadly, he only built two – one for himself and one for the Queen. For most people, toilets stayed in the Dark Ages.

John Harington's toilet had a water-filled box or cistern, like a modern toilet.

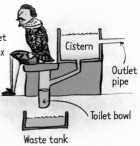

Cistern

Outlet pipe

Toilet bowl

Waste tank

Around the bend

After Harington, little happened in toilet history until 1775. Then, English watchmaker Alexander Cummings invented a toilet with a brilliant new feature: the S-bend. Before this, waste fell straight down into a sewage tank or channel – and stinky smells could easily waft back up. The S-bend used a curved pipe to trap some clean water, sealing the toilet off from the smelly sewers beneath.

From then on, toilets took off, and many inventors came up with improved versions – although modern toilets still have the same basic design, with a cistern and an S-bend.

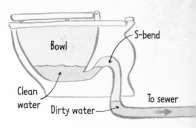

After the toilet is flushed, some water is trapped in the bend and in the bowl, sealing it from the sewer. The S-bend is simply an S-shaped curve in the pipe, or siphon, leading out of the toilet bowl.

Dirt and disease

In the 1800s, scientists realized that germs from human waste could spread diseases. Governments soon began building sewer systems and installing toilets everywhere so that the germs could be safely flushed away.

Toilets were made of wood and metal until 1885, when Thomas Twyford invented an all-in-one toilet bowl and siphon made from porcelain.

What about Crapper?

Many people think that a man named Thomas Crapper invented the flushing toilet, but he didn't. Crapper was a British businessman who supplied toilets to the rich and famous in the late 1800s. His business brochures suggested that he had invented the toilet, but in fact he'd only come up with a few minor improvements.

Toilet paper
People have used all sorts of things as toilet paper – leaves, grass, corn cobs, sponges and newspaper. The first specially made toilet paper was invented in the US in 1857, by Joseph C. Gayetty. It was softened with aloe gel and had Gayetty's name printed on every sheet.

Talking toilets

Some toilets now have speakers built into them. They can welcome you to the bathroom, remind you to wash your hands, or play some music for you.

Toilet paper was first sold on a roll in 1880.

Don't forget to flush!

Bright ideas

When it's too dark to read, you just flick a switch, and light fills the room – thanks to the lightbulb. But this brilliant invention took many years to perfect.

The first electric lights

English scientist Humphry Davy first made an electric light in 1801. He ran electricity through a platinum strip, making it glow. But it wasn't practical, as the strip soon burned away to nothing – and platinum is very expensive. In 1809, Davy invented another electric light, the arc lamp, in which an electric current jumped across a gap, making the air glow. Arc lamps worked, but they were too big, hot and smelly to use at home.

For years, inventors tried to come up with a small, long-life electric light. Many say the first true lightbulb was invented by a German inventor, Heinrich Göbel, in 1854, but it was never developed for everyday use.

Davy found that running electricity through a strip of platinum would make it glow with light.

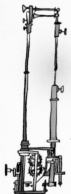

The arc lamp created light by making electricity jump across a narrow gap in a circuit.

Heinrich Göbel

why a bulb?
A lightbulb has a strip or "filament" that gives out light when electricity runs through it. In air, the filament soon burns away. It lasts longer if it's surrounded by other gases, or a vacuum (an empty space). So the filament needs to be inside a sealed glass bulb to keep the air out.

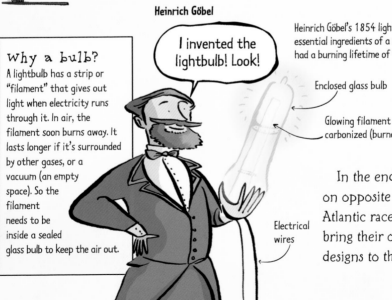

I invented the lightbulb! Look!

Heinrich Göbel's 1854 lightbulb had all the essential ingredients of a modern bulb, and had a burning lifetime of 400 hours.

Enclosed glass bulb

Glowing filament made from carbonized (burned) bamboo

Electrical wires

In the end, two inventors on opposite sides of the Atlantic raced each other to bring their own lightbulb designs to the public.

I invented the lightbulb!!

Joseph Swan

No, I invented the lightbulb!!!

Thomas Edison

Swan and Edison came up with very similar lightbulb designs.

Swan versus Edison

Around 1850, an English scientist, Joseph Swan, began work on his lightbulb. He used a carbonized thread filament inside a vacuum-filled bulb. But it took years to get a really good vacuum inside the bulb. Finally, in 1878, Swan patented his lightbulb and demonstrated it to the public.

But that same year, the great US inventor Thomas Edison had set to work on the lightbulb too. He came up with a similar design to Swan's, and patented it in America in 1879.

Lighting the world

In 1880, Edison equipped a steam ship, the "Columbia," with electric lighting, and in 1881 he began to supply buildings in New York City too. Back in Britain, Swan brought electric light to the Houses of Parliament in London in 1881 and the British Museum in 1882.

At first, Edison and Swan argued over who had really invented the lightbulb. But in 1882 they went into business together, and formed the Edison & Swan United Company to make and sell lightbulbs and lamps.

New York was one of the first cities to be lit by lightbulbs.

Fluorescent bulbs

Another type of lightbulb is the fluorescent bulb, perfected by German inventor Edmund Germer in 1926. This is a glass tube full of gases that give out ultraviolet (UV) light when electricity flows through them. Though UV light is invisible, the tube has a fluorescent coating that glows when the UV light hits it. Modern low-energy lightbulbs work this way.

Traditional lightbulb

Some modern lightbulbs still work in the same way as early bulbs. But many people are now switching to low-energy lightbulbs, which make less heat and so save energy.

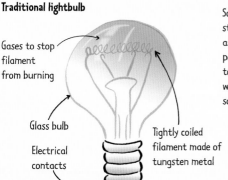

Gases to stop filament from burning

Glass bulb

Electrical contacts

Tightly coiled filament made of tungsten metal

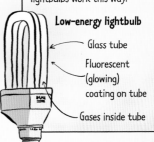

Low-energy lightbulb

Glass tube

Fluorescent (glowing) coating on tube

Gases inside tube

Electrical contacts

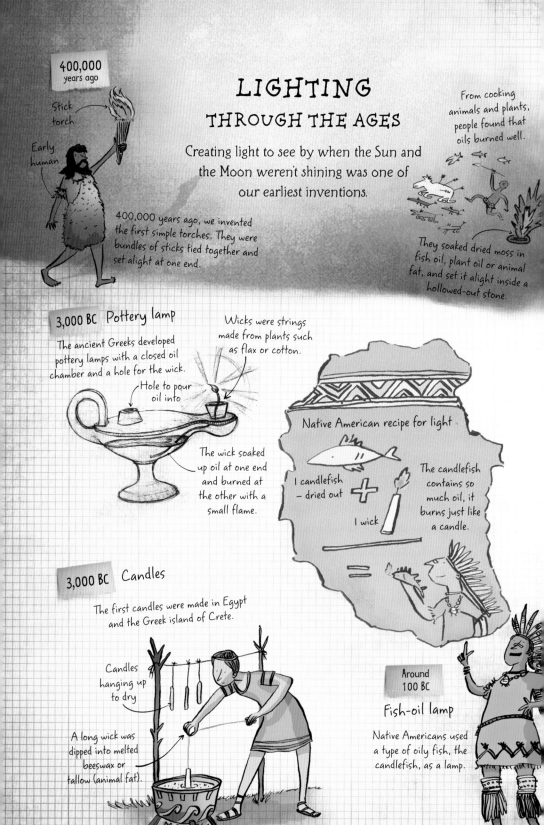

LIGHTING
THROUGH THE AGES

Creating light to see by when the Sun and the Moon weren't shining was one of our earliest inventions.

400,000 years ago

Stick torch

Early human

400,000 years ago, we invented the first simple torches. They were bundles of sticks tied together and set alight at one end.

From cooking animals and plants, people found that oils burned well.

They soaked dried moss in fish oil, plant oil or animal fat, and set it alight inside a hollowed-out stone.

3,000 BC Pottery lamp

The ancient Greeks developed pottery lamps with a closed oil chamber and a hole for the wick.

Wicks were strings made from plants such as flax or cotton.

Hole to pour oil into

The wick soaked up oil at one end and burned at the other with a small flame.

Native American recipe for light

1 candlefish – dried out

1 wick

The candlefish contains so much oil, it burns just like a candle.

3,000 BC Candles

The first candles were made in Egypt and the Greek island of Crete.

Candles hanging up to dry

A long wick was dipped into melted beeswax or tallow (animal fat).

Around 100 BC

Fish-oil lamp

Native Americans used a type of oily fish, the candlefish, as a lamp.

Argand lamp

Gas lighting

In the 1780s, Swiss chemist Aimé Argand improved on simple oil lamps by adding three things...

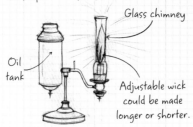

Glass chimney

Oil tank

Adjustable wick could be made longer or shorter.

...making his "Argand lamp" much brighter than a basic oil lamp.

Gas lighting dates from 1792, when Scottish inventor William Murdoch used it to light his own home.

Soon, gas was being used to light whole buildings and cities.

A lamplighter would light the gas lamps every evening, and put them out in the morning.

I've seen the light!

1809 Electric light

The first ever electric light was the arc light, invented by British inventor Humphry Davy in 1809.

Ooooh!

Aaaaaaaah!

An electric current was forced across a gap in an electric circuit, making a glowing line or "arc" of light.

After lightbulbs were patented in the 1870s, electric lighting took over the world.

1965

LEDs, or light-emitting diodes, were invented in 1965. These low-energy, long-lasting, very small bulbs can give out colored light.

We now have many kinds of lighting, including battery-run flashlights.

Cell phone

The little flashing lights on electronic gadgets are LEDs.

LEDs are made of SEMICONDUCTORS – special metals that give out colored light when electricity flows through them.

Some road signs and traffic lights are made of LEDS.

TV remote control

The word "telephone" – from the Greek for "distant sound" – existed before Bell's invention. Until 1876, it meant any sound that carried a long way, such as a foghorn.

Inventing the telephone

Alexander Graham Bell is famous for inventing the telephone. In fact, many inventors came up with similar ideas, but Bell's was the first working telephone to be fully patented.

Messages by wire

In 1870s Boston, USA, Scottish-born inventor Alexander Graham Bell was working on improving the telegraph. This was an invention that used wires to carry long-distance, coded messages in the form of electrical signals. Bell hoped to find a way to send several signals at once. But, in 1874, his experiments gave him another idea. He saw how he might be able to turn the human voice into an electrical signal, and send that along a wire instead.

Bell and his assistant Thomas Watson worked on this idea for months, in secret. By the summer of 1875 they had managed to send some muffled sounds along a wire.

Alexander Graham Bell examines his first telephone with his assistant, Thomas Watson.

Several inventors were working on telephone designs at around the same time. For example, Johann Philipp Reis's telephone, invented in 1860, was very quiet and muffled, but it did transmit sounds.

Patent race

Bell's telephone couldn't yet transmit speech clearly, but on February 14 1876, he submitted a patent application. On the same day, two hours earlier, another inventor, Elisha Gray, submitted a "caveat" – a note of his intention to file a patent – for his own telephone design. But Bell's paperwork was dealt with first, and appeared first in the log book. Gray later challenged Bell's patent, but Bell won. So he went down in history as the inventor of the telephone.

Bell's telephone

The key to making the telephone work lay in converting the varying sounds of speech into a varying electric current. Here's how Bell did this:

1. This cone collected sound waves – vibrations in the air made by speaking.

2. The vibrations made this thin membrane vibrate up and down.

3. The vibrating membrane made this needle move up and down too.

4. The moving needle was held in a container full of acid. As it moved up and down, it changed how well the acid could conduct (carry) a flow of electricity.

5. The acid was part of a circuit carrying an electric current. As the conductivity of the acid changed, the current in the circuit varied.

6. The circuit carried the varying signal along a wire to another telephone, where the process was reversed.

7. The transmitted speech came out here.

"Watson, come here!"

Bell kept improving his telephone until it worked well. On March 10 1876, as Thomas Watson tested the receiver in another room, Bell made his famous first phone call: "Mr. Watson, come here. I want to see you."

> Mr. Watson, come here. I want to see you!

Telephones today

Landline telephones today work just like Bell's telephone, by turning sound vibrations into a varying electrical current – although they have modern electronic parts instead of acid and a needle. But many people nowadays use cell phones, which work another way – using radio waves.

A cell phone is a mini radio set. It converts your voice vibrations into radio signals.

The nearest base tower collects the signals and sends them to their destination on a traditional landline.

Another base tower transmits radio signals to send your call to another cell phone.

A record of sound

Today, if you want to listen to music, you just spin a CD or turn on your MP3 player. But 150 years ago, there was no such thing. Music was live, and that was it. Until, that is, a great inventor tried to record sound...

The great inventor

Thomas Edison was a telegraph operator who designed many improvements to the telegraph (see page 42). By 1874, he'd made enough money to set up an invention lab in New Jersey, USA. Edison invented over 1,000 things, including modern lightbulbs (see page 38).

Voice vibrations

In 1876, the telephone was invented. It worked by turning the sound of a human voice into vibrations in a thin, flexible disc. Edison wondered if the vibrations in the disc could somehow be stored.

What is sound?

Sound is made when an object vibrates (moves quickly back and forth). For example, when you hit a drum, it vibrates. This makes air particles vibrate too. The vibrations spread through the air as sound waves, which our ears can detect.

Sound waves in the air, made up of vibrating particles.

Ear detects vibrations.

Vibrating object

In his work with the telegraph, Edison recorded messages as a series of indentations on special tape called ticker tape.

Hmmm... I wonder...?

The moving needle writes...

Edison took a telephone mouthpiece and attached a needle to the disc part. When he spoke into the mouthpiece, the disc vibrated, and so did the needle. He used the vibrating needle to scratch a pattern on a strip of paper. This did make a record of the vibrations — but it couldn't be played back.

A pattern of marks on the tape represented words.

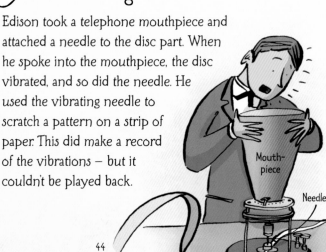

Mouth-piece

Needle

Get into the groove

Then Edison had another great idea — using tin foil instead of paper. If the needle rested against a spinning, foil-covered cylinder, it would make a groove in the foil. The vibration of the needle would be recorded as a pattern of ripples in the groove.

Now for the brainwave. Edison realized that you could reverse the whole process. If the needle was drawn through the groove again, it would make the disc vibrate in exactly the same pattern as when the sound was recorded.

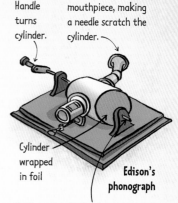

Handle turns cylinder.

Operator speaks into mouthpiece, making a needle scratch the cylinder.

Cylinder wrapped in foil

Edison's phonograph

Shaft moves cylinder along as it spins, so the needle cuts a spiral groove.

Playback time

Edison had had the idea, but he hadn't made the machine or tested it. He sketched what it should look like and gave the sketch to an employee at his lab, John Kreusi, to build.

As soon as it was ready, Edison tried it out. Winding the cylinder around and around, he spoke the words: "Mary had a little lamb," as the needle scratched a groove. He placed the needle back in the groove, wound again, and was amazed to hear his own voice being played back to him.

Mary had a little lamb

Sounds on wax

Edison named his invention the phonograph (meaning "sound-writing"). It was a brilliant idea, but there was still some work to do. The foil wore out and tore, so he developed cylinders with a hard wax coating instead. One cylinder could record four minutes of speech, or two minutes of music.

By 1900, after adding more improvements, Edison was selling phonographs and cylinder records to the public.

Wealthy people enjoyed listening to opera on cylinder phonographs.

45

Berliner's first gramophone

The first flat records were made of glass. Later they were made of zinc, then plastic.

A flat record has a spiral groove running from the outer edge toward the middle.

Going flat

In 1877, ten years after the phonograph was invented, German-born inventor Emile Berliner came up with a new idea. He found a way to record sound onto flat discs instead of cylinders. His recording device was known as the gramophone. Edison continued to make cylinder records for many years, but eventually, Berliner's flat records became much more popular.

New inventions

The flat gramophone record dominated the 20th century recording industry. Berliner's discs gave rise to the terms "disc jockey" (or DJ) and "disco." Flat, grooved records are still used today – especially for scratching and mixing. But there have also been many new sound recording inventions...

All kinds of uses

Edison saw at once how useful his invention could be. He wrote an essay about it in 1878, listing all the things the phonograph could be useful for, including:

- Dictation to record letters and ideas
- Talking books and talking clocks for the blind
- Educational materials
- Records of phone calls
- Music boxes and toys
- Musical recordings

All these are important uses of sound recording today, over 100 years later.

- In 1928, German scientist Fritz Pfleumer invented a simple way of recording sound onto tape covered in magnetic particles.

Audiotape cassette

Indentations ("pits") in CD

- In 1965, US inventor James Russell invented the CD (Compact Disc). It records sound as a series of pits read by a beam of light.

- Sound can now also be recorded directly onto computer memory, and stored in an MP3 player.

MP3 player

Television is born

Television is one of the most important modern inventions. It brings entertainment, education and news into our homes every day. But TV is complicated. It took more than one brilliant mind to invent it.

A name for TV
For years before TV was invented, people dreamed of being able to send moving pictures long-distance. They came up with all kinds of futuristic names for this hi-tech idea...

Light into electricity

Television works by turning patterns of light into electrical signals. In 1839, Edmond Becquerel found that shining light onto some types of metal creates an electric current. This led to the invention of the photo-voltaic cell, which turns light into electricity. Becquerel had taken the first step toward inventing the television.

Optiphone! Phototelegraphy! Mirascope! Farscope! Radioscope!

The word that finally caught on – "television" – was made up in about 1900, over 20 years before TV actually existed. It comes from the Greek word "tele," meaning distant, and the Latin word "visio," meaning sight.

Scanning moving pictures

On Christmas Eve, 1883, a German science student named Paul Nipkow had an idea for a machine that could scan moving images and turn them into a series of signals. His invention was the Nipkow disc. It was a simple disc with holes in it, arranged in a spiral. Here's how it worked:

Nipkow disc

1. The disc spins very fast in front of a moving object.

3. As the disc spins, the holes pass in front of the image. Each hole records a slice of the moving image as a flashing pattern of light and dark.

5. If the same light patterns shine through another spinning Nipkow disc, the moving image reforms and can be seen on a screen.

Light

Moving object

2. Light from the object hits the disc and patterns of light shine through the holes.

Photovoltaic cell

Light

4. The light patterns are collected by a photovoltaic cell and turned into a series of electrical signals.

Glass Screen

47

Rosing's early TV system only transmitted simple black and white silhouette images of geometric shapes.

Crazy inventor

John Logie Baird came up with many madcap ideas. He designed air-soled shoes, socks that kept your feet dry, and a non-rusting razor made of glass, with which he cut himself badly. And while building his television, Baird almost died when he accidentally gave himself a 2,000-volt electric shock.

The television trail

In the early 1900s, many inventors tried to build working televisions that could actually send moving pictures long-distance. The first to succeed was probably Russian scientist Boris Rosing. In 1907 he made a television using a Nipkow disc. But he only managed to transmit still silhouettes. The first inventor to build a TV and use it to send an actual moving image was a Scotsman, John Logie Baird.

John Logie Baird

Today, many people think of John Logie Baird as the true inventor of television — although his system was soon replaced by improved versions designed by other inventors. Baird built his TV system in his attic. It was based on the Nipkow disc, and made of household objects. Finally, on Friday October 31, 1925, he managed to get his TV to work for the first time.

John Logie Baird's prototype television

Baird's system used spinning discs to turn light patterns into electrical signals. The signals could be sent along a wire, or carried by radio waves.

1. Strong light illuminates the subject.

2. Grid divides light from the subject into sections.

Slots in revolving disc

5. Transmitter turns electrical signals into radio signals.

Motor

3. These two discs together work like a Nipkow disc, translating a moving image into a flickering light pattern.

4. Photovoltaic cell turns light patterns into electrical signals.

Going public

By 1926, Baird was demonstrating his TV to the public in Selfridges department store in London. In 1928, he successfully sent a TV signal between London and New York, and in 1929 the BBC (British Broadcasting Corporation), which already broadcast radio shows, began using Baird's television system to broadcast TV shows.

Early TV sets had a tiny black-and-white screen set into a huge box.

Better versions

Of course, TVs today don't look anything like Baird's contraption. Soon after he made his breakthrough, other scientists made improved TV systems using a device called a cathode ray tube. This creates an image on a screen using a beam of tiny particles called electrons, without the need for a big spinning disc. Eventually, the BBC switched to this method, and it became the basis of modern TV broadcasting and viewing.

For most of the 20th century, TVs were bulky because of the large cathode ray tube behind the screen.

In the 1990s, LCD (liquid crystal display) screens replaced TVs that have cathode ray tubes, and flat televisions became available.

9. At the receiving end, another disc turns the flickering light patterns back into a moving image.

8. Electrical signals make a neon tube light bulb glow in a flickering pattern.

10. Moving image appears on a screen.

Antenna   Light bulb

7. Radio signals can travel any distance before being collected and turned back into electrical signals.

Revolving disc

49

The computer age

Computers are a huge part of modern life, and most of us use them every day. Yet the computer was never really "invented" — it developed gradually. No single inventor thought it up.

Mathematical machines

Roman boys used abacuses to learn mathematics at school. The abacus is a simple calculating machine — an early version of the computer.

A computer is basically a machine that computes. That means it takes in numbers, does mathematical calculations on them and gives out the results. In some ways it's just a much more complicated version of the abacus — a set of beads on a wooden frame. By moving the beads, you can store numbers and do calculations. People were using abacuses in Babylonia (in what is now Iraq) up to 3,000 years ago, and in some places they still do.

From the 1600s, inventors began to develop more complex calculating machines. The most important was the analytical engine, designed by English mathematician Charles Babbage in the 1840s. He never finished building it, but it was the forerunner of modern computers. Unlike an abacus, the analytical engine could follow a set of instructions — a computer program.

If he had completed it, Babbage's analytical engine would have looked like this. It was steam-powered and worked using wheels and cogs.

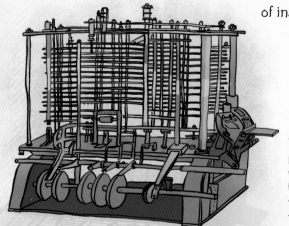

Ada Lovelace, the daughter of the great poet Lord Byron, created programs for the engine. She is now remembered as the first computer programmer.

The first computer programs were cards with patterns of holes punched in them, designed to be fed into the machine.

Electric computers

Babbage's work was forgotten for a while. But during the Second World War, governments needed computers to crack codes and plot missile paths. Instead of using cogs and wheels, inventors designed new electric computers that used devices called vacuum tubes. A flow of electricity through each tube could set it to an "on" or "off" position, allowing the tubes to store and process numbers.

ENIAC took up as much space as 5 modern school classrooms, and contained over 17,000 vacuum tubes.

The first fully functioning, digital, programmable vacuum-tube computer was called ENIAC (Electronic Numerical Integrator And Computer). It was designed and built by two US scientists, John Mauchly and J. Presper Eckert, from 1943 to 1946.

Getting smaller

In 1947, US scientists Walter Brattain and John Bardeen invented the transistor, a kind of tiny electronic switch. Transistors were soon used to replace bulky vacuum tubes in computers. This made computers much smaller.

A silicon chip

They became smaller still when Jack Kilby and Robert Noyce invented the integrated circuit, or silicon chip, in 1958. Instead of being made up of lots of separate transistors, a computer's electrical circuits could be fit onto a tiny slice, or chip, of the mineral silicon.

Computers for the people

Gradually, computers became small and cheap enough to be used in offices, and then at home. The MITS Altair 8800, launched in 1975, was the first home computer. Today, most homes have at least one computer.

On the move
Computers can now be made small enough to carry around in a bag or even a pocket. Laptop or notebook computers have their circuits and chips hidden under the keyboard and are no bigger than an abacus.

COMMUNICATIONS
THROUGH THE AGES

Sending messages has always been important to people. And over the years, we've figured out more and more ways to send messages faster and further.

1000 BC First postal service

Persian on horseback

The first postal services used messengers on horseback to pass on packages and letters.

700 BC Scytale

Beginning around 700 BC, the Greeks used a kind of stick called a SCYTALE to send coded messages. It was very handy for sending secret instructions in wartime.

776 BC Carrier pigeons

The ancient Egyptians, Greeks and Romans used pigeons to carry messages.

Messages were tied to the pigeon's foot.

Pentathlon Winner   Pythos

Pigeons were used to send news from the Olympic Games to the city of Athens.

To encode a message, the Greeks wrapped a leather strip around the scytale, then wrote words along it.

A messenger delivered the strip to its destination. There, it was wrapped around a matching scytale to reveal the message.

By the 2nd century Smoke signals

Native American sending a smoke message

The ancient Chinese and native Americans used fires and smoke signals to send simple messages, such as "All is well" or "Send help!"

1430s Printing press

The invention of the printing press in the 1430s led to mass-produced books.

A Gutenberg printing press from the 1400s

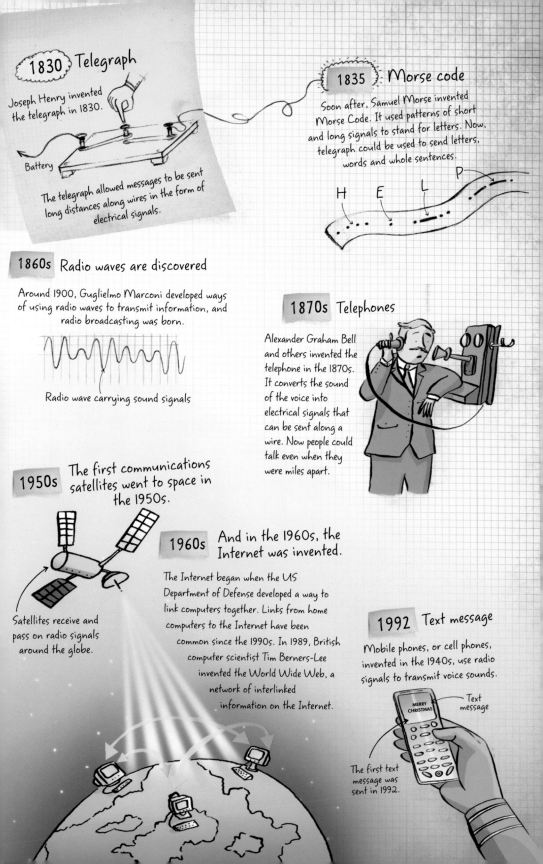

1830 Telegraph

Joseph Henry invented the telegraph in 1830.

Battery

The telegraph allowed messages to be sent long distances along wires in the form of electrical signals.

1835 Morse code

Soon after, Samuel Morse invented Morse Code. It used patterns of short and long signals to stand for letters. Now, telegraph could be used to send letters, words and whole sentences.

H E L P

1860s Radio waves are discovered

Around 1900, Guglielmo Marconi developed ways of using radio waves to transmit information, and radio broadcasting was born.

Radio wave carrying sound signals

1870s Telephones

Alexander Graham Bell and others invented the telephone in the 1870s. It converts the sound of the voice into electrical signals that can be sent along a wire. Now people could talk even when they were miles apart.

1950s The first communications satellites went to space in the 1950s.

Satellites receive and pass on radio signals around the globe.

1960s And in the 1960s, the Internet was invented.

The Internet began when the US Department of Defense developed a way to link computers together. Links from home computers to the Internet have been common since the 1990s. In 1989, British computer scientist Tim Berners-Lee invented the World Wide Web, a network of interlinked information on the Internet.

1992 Text message

Mobile phones, or cell phones, invented in the 1940s, use radio signals to transmit voice sounds.

MERRY CHRISTMAS

Text message

The first text message was sent in 1992.

The story of jeans

You probably own at least one pair of jeans. And so does everyone you know. They're the most popular clothes on Earth. So where did jeans come from?

Setting up shop

In the 1840s, Levi Strauss, a German-born tailor, went to the USA to make his fortune. After arriving in New York, he moved to San Francisco, where he opened a wholesale warehouse. His business, called Levi Strauss & Co., sold things like clothing, bed sheets, ribbons and fabric. Stores all over the state of California bought items from Strauss and sold them on to their own customers. Others bought supplies which they used to make their own goods.

Tough trousers

Why "denim"?
Denim probably got its name from the French town of Nîmes, where it was first made. It became known as "serge de Nîmes." But in English, this was shortened to "denim."

It was the time of the Gold Rush, when thousands of treasure-hunters went searching for gold in California's hills. It was hard, dirty work, and they needed tough outdoor clothes. Most of these gold-diggers wore hard-wearing pants known as waist overalls, made from denim. One of the things Strauss sold in his warehouse was denim fabric.

One day in 1872, Levi Strauss received an interesting letter. It was from Jacob Davis, one of his customers. Davis was a tailor. He bought fabric from Strauss and used it to make overalls. He had designed a brand-new type of work pants, held together with copper rivets to make them extra strong. He wanted to go into business with Strauss to set up a factory to make them.

Is this my lucky day?

Waist overalls were plain, baggy denim pants.

Pants partnership

After reading the letter, Strauss agreed to work with Jacob Davis. In 1873, they patented Davis's design for pants with copper rivets, and opened two factories to manufacture them.

Soon, they were in production, making the riveted pants in two colors: brown cotton duck (a heavy fabric like canvas) and blue denim. The brown ones sold quite well. But the blue denim pants were an instant hit. They sold out immediately.

The people's pants

The riveted denims were so popular, Strauss and Davis had to set up new factories to make more and more of them. By the 1880s, people all over the American West were wearing Levi's® brand blue denim riveted waist overalls. As well as wearing them for work, people started wearing them to look good.

Going global

Thanks to the Hollywood film industry, people all around the world saw popular movie stars wearing Levi's® jeans in Westerns. And during the Second World War, people around the world saw American servicemen wearing them. Before long, everyone wanted a pair! By the 1950s, jeans were being sold all over the USA. They eventually spread to the rest of the world. Today, you can buy jeans almost everywhere on the planet.

Davis's design used rivets to hold the fabric together. The rivets stopped the pants from falling apart with heavy use.

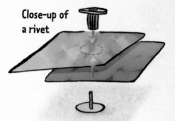

Close-up of a rivet

Levi and Davis made their pants with orange stitching to match the copper rivets.

> ### Why "jeans"?
> Blue denim pants became known as "jeans" in the 1950s, but no one is sure why. It could be because people used to wear pants made of a fabric called jean — and so the name "jeans" ended up being used for other pants, too.

THEY ATTACKED AT DAWN

Arrgh! Stupid boots!

Zip it up!

Buttons, belts, clasps, laces, hooks and eyes... there have always been plenty of time-consuming, fiddly ways to fasten your clothes. So inventors invented the zipper to make the whole process quicker and easier.

Boot bother

Boots used to be done up with laces, or hooks and eyes. But, in 1890, inventor Whitcomb Judson, of Chicago, USA, decided to find a better way. A friend of his had moaned that doing up all the bothersome fastenings on his boots made his back ache.

So Judson invented a fastener made of two rows of hooks and eyes, that could fit into each other when they were pressed together. He also designed a special slider, which moved along the two rows and pushed them together, joining them automatically.

Into business

Judson patented his device in 1893, calling it a "clasp locker." Then he set up a company, the Universal Fastener Company, to try to sell it. But the clasp locker didn't really catch on.

One problem was that it wasn't very strong — it would just pop apart. Judson designed a new improved version, the C-curity, in 1904, but it still wasn't a great success.

Judson's first "clasp locker" design could be sewed onto boots or clothes.

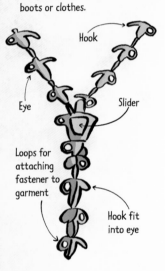

Hook

Eye

Slider

Loops for attaching fastener to garment

Hook fit into eye

Early bird

Like so many inventions, zippers were actually first thought of much earlier. Elias Howe, who also invented the sewing machine, had an idea for a zipper-like fastener in 1851. But, being busy with his sewing machine, he never developed it.

The C-curity was attached to its own cloth edging.

Look - no hooks!

Eventually, Judson's company hired a Swedish scientist, Gideon Sundback, to work on the C-curity. He went back to the drawing board, and came up with his new invention – the "hookless fastener" – in 1913.

Instead of hooks and eyes, Sundback used tiny "scoops," with a bump on one side and a hollow on the other. The slider squeezed the scoops together so that they interlocked. He also designed a machine to make the scoops and attach them to fabric strips.

Sundback's hookless fastener looked pretty much like a modern zipper. Its breakthrough design made the zipper a household object.

The design had more fasteners than Judson's – about 4 per cm (11 per inch) – making it stronger.

Zipper boots

The Universal Fastener Company became the Hookless Fastener Company, and set out to sell the new fasteners.

At first only the army and navy wanted them, for bags and flying suits. Then, in 1921, rubber company BF Goodrich ordered thousands of hookless fasteners for a new rubber boot, called the "zipper" boot. The name was soon used for the fastener itself – probably because of the noise it made.

Flying suit

Zip-up boots

Sundback's "scoops" were like tiny spoons. Today we call them "teeth."

The bumps and hollows were rectangle-shaped. This stopped the scoops from twisting around and popping the fastener open.

Zippers for nippers

In the 1930s, zippers were marketed for children's clothes, because they were easy to do up and helped small children to dress themselves.

Before long, zippers were being used on all kinds of clothes. And today, of course, they're found on hundreds of other things too, from tents to CD cases.

Ick! Those sticky burrs again...!

Hooks and loops

"**R**rriipp!!" A sound you'll hear coming from clothes, bags, shoes and countless other things with hook-and-loop fasteners. This amazingly useful invention began with a single, brilliant idea — and it was copied from nature.

Mestral in the mountains

It was 1941, and Georges de Mestral was walking in the mountains with his dog.

Mestral, a Swiss engineer, loved the outdoors. The only problem was that when he got home after a walk, his clothes and his dog were covered with annoying burrs — tiny, sticky, ball-shaped seed pods that come from some types of plants.

Mestral had always been a thinker and inventor — he had invented and patented a toy plane when he was 12 — and he wanted to know how the burrs worked. So he took a look at them under a microscope.

There, he saw that each tiny burr was covered in even smaller hairs, shaped like miniature hooks. This explained how the burrs managed to cling so tightly to the dog's hair and Mestral's clothes. Even though each hook on its own was quite weak, hundreds of them working together made the burrs hold themselves fast to any soft fur or fabric.

Mestral saw that each burr was covered with tiny hook-shaped hairs.

The hairs hooked onto his dog's fur and his wool walking gear.

why have burrs?
We know why we want to stick things together — but why do plants have sticky burrs? It's because they need to spread out, or disperse, their seeds. The burrs contain the plant's seeds. They stick onto animals and the seeds get carried far away, to grow in new areas.

Fuss-free fastener

Mestral had an idea. He could design a man-made fastener that would work just like the burrs! He hated awkward buttons and zippers that broke, so he knew that if he could make his fastener work, it would be in demand.

Getting started

Mestral went to visit fabric companies to see if they could make the materials he needed. The fastener had to have two sides – one covered with soft loops, the other with strong, very small hooks.

The soft side wasn't too hard to make. But it took more than eight years of working with fabric makers in Lyon, France and Basle, Switzerland, until Mestral found the best way to manufacture the hooked part.

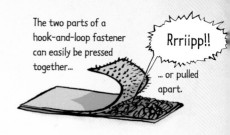

The two parts of a hook-and-loop fastener can easily be pressed together...

Rrriipp!!

... or pulled apart.

The hooked side of the fastener is made by sewing tiny strands of nylon plastic into strong cotton tape.

The soft side is made of loosely looped, woven nylon.

An astronaut in zero gravity

Tools can be attached to strips of fastener on the astronaut's suit.

Hook-and-loop fasteners stop food bags from floating away.

Finding a name

Mestral patented his invention in 1951, and set up the Velcro companies to make and sell it. The name "velcro" came from two French words: "velour," meaning velvet (the soft side), and "crochet," meaning hook.

At first, people were reluctant to use Velcro® brand hook-and-loop fasteners on everyday clothes. But they were a hit with the fast-growing space industry. They were ideal for making easy-to-fasten space suits, and for holding things (and people) down in the weightlessness of space.

Gradually, manufacturers began putting hook-and-loop fasteners on children's clothes and shoes, as they were easy to use – and they soon caught on for everyday items, too.

Fastener facts
- A typical piece of Velcro® brand hook-and-loop fastener has 400 hooks per square inch (62 per square cm).
- The product comes in many varieties – and there is even a metal-coated version that can conduct electricity.
- If a hook-and-loop fastener is shaken, it sticks more tightly. This makes it good for holding together car parts.

This wall-jumping game involves leaping onto a wall wearing a suit covered in hook-and-loop fastener.

Surgery without tears

People have been doing operations for thousands of years. At first, they tried to cure illnesses by making holes in each other's skulls to let out evil spirits. And if your arm or leg was crushed or diseased, you could have it cut off.

But there haven't always been good anaesthetics — drugs for numbing pain during surgery. Having an operation used to mean horrible agony. Operating rooms echoed to the sounds of patients' screams and groans.

It's a knockout!

Knocking patients unconscious could cause dangerous injuries.

Of course, doctors wanted to make surgery less painful. They tried knocking patients out cold, getting them drunk, giving them leather to chew on, and even stinging them with nettles to distract them. But none of these was really the answer.

What a gas!

Getting them drunk was risky too – some died of alcohol poisoning.

Then, in the 1700s, scientists began learning how to mix up different gases. Around 1800, inventor Humphry Davy experimented with a gas called nitrous oxide. When he breathed it in, it made him laugh his head off, then fall over. So he called it "laughing gas."

Ha ha ha ha haaa!

And stinging nettles only made operations an even worse experience.

Party time!

Davy began holding laughing gas parties where everyone laughed all night long. Soon, people began to notice that the gas numbed pain, too.

When dentists realized this, they decided to try out laughing gas on their patients. One dentist named Horace Wells took the gas and asked a friend to pull his tooth out. It worked!

I didn't feel a thing!

Laughing gas bag

Ether

Unfortunately, laughing gas only had an effect for a short time. It was fine for pulling out a tooth, but not for longer operations. So dentists tried a liquid called ether instead. Sniffing ether-soaked rags knocked patients out and numbed pain.

There was just one problem – ether was an explosive. Using it too close to candles led to some nasty accidents.

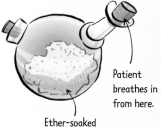

Dr. William Morton invented an ether inhaler for his patients to use.

Patient breathes in from here.

Ether-soaked rags go in here.

Simpson's solution

In the 1840s, a Scottish doctor, James Simpson, found that a liquid called chloroform worked just as well as ether, and was much safer. His female patients were delighted when he used chloroform to save them from the pain of childbirth.

Some religious people said numbing pain was wrong. "Suffering is right and natural!" they cried. But Queen Victoria put a stop to that when she used chloroform herself in 1853. Then everyone wanted to try it.

Today, scientists have built on the work of Davy, Wells and Simpson to make many more kinds of anaesthetics. So if you ever need an operation, it should be painless!

One gives anaesthetic one's royal approval!

Spectacular specs

Over 2,000 years ago, the ancient Chinese made the first eye glasses. But they didn't improve your eyesight – they just shielded your eyes from the Sun. Actual glasses only came along centuries later. In the ancient world, people just had to put up with bad eyesight. Near-sighted Romans made their slaves read to them. As for the slaves, if they had bad eyesight, they were sold off cheap.

Lenses and light

A lens is a curved piece of glass. As light rays pass through it, they bend.

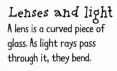

Light rays

Lens

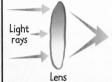

The eye has a curved cornea (covering) and a jelly-like lens inside. These both bend light and focus it on the retina at the back of the eyeball, making a sharp image.

Seeing the light

In about 1020, an Arabic scientist, Alhazen, studied lenses (curved pieces of glass). He saw that light would bend as it passed through a lens. If you saw objects through some types of lenses, they looked bigger.

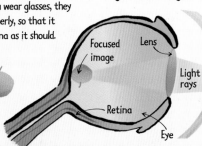

Before long, monks in Europe (who read a lot) began using lenses called reading stones to make reading easier. You moved the "stone" (really a curved piece of glass) over the page, and it made the letters look bigger. It was a kind of early magnifying glass.

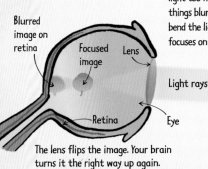

Near-sightedness (myopia)

Blurred image on retina

Focused image

Lens

Retina

Eye

The lens flips the image. Your brain turns it the right way up again.

If you have myopia, your eye lenses bend light too much, which makes far off things blurry. If you wear glasses, they bend the light properly, so that it focuses on the retina as it should.

Correction of near-sightedness using a lens

Concave spectacle lens helps to bend light rays.

Focused image

Lens

Light rays

Retina

Eye

Glasses are born

In 1268, English scholar Roger Bacon wrote about
how lenses could be put in front of the eyes to
correct bad eyesight. But he didn't bother turning
his idea into reality.

The first eye glasses were probably made in
Italy in around 1280. No one knows who made
them first, though Salvino degli Armati of Florence
and Alessandro della Spina of Pisa both designed
early versions. Either way, specs were a hit. By
1300, thousands of pairs were being made.

In the 1300s, glasses began to
appear in paintings, such as this
church frieze in Treviso, Italy.

What were they like?

The first glasses were made of two lenses in metal
frames, joined by a folding hinge or a springy wire.
They didn't have ear hooks – you just clamped them
around your nose.

Early specs like these, with no
ear hooks, are sometimes called
"nose spectacles."

Hinged nose
spectacles

At first, glasses only worked for far-sightedness (when
you can't see things close to your face). They were useful
for reading, writing and craft work. But ever since then,
inventors have been improving on glasses:

Springy nose
spectacles

• 1400s Different types of lenses were used to make
glasses for near-sighted people...
• 1784 American Benjamin Franklin invented
bifocals – glasses with two types of lens in one...
• 1888 Swiss scientist A. Eugene Fick invented
contact lenses, which sit right on the eyeball...
• ...and since the 1980s, you can actually have
an operation on the lenses in your eyes
instead. The surgeon uses a laser to reshape
the lens so that it focuses more sharply.

Laser eye treatment

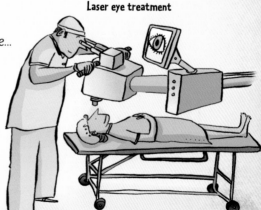

Ouch! Not again!

The story of adhesive bandage

When you cut your finger or scrape your knee, you stick a bandage on it. But who thought of adhesive bandages? It was a man named Earle Dickson, who came up with the idea thanks to his clumsy wife.

All fingers and thumbs

Joseph Lister

So, in 1885, Robert Wood Johnson and his brothers started a business making sterile bandages. Today, their company, Johnson & Johnson, makes many healthcare products and is one of the world's best-known companies.

In 1920, American Earle Dickson was working for the Johnson & Johnson company, which made bandages and dressings for hospitals. He often took dressings home for his wife, Josephine. She was a housewife and she was always cutting and burning her hands and fingers while doing the cooking and cleaning.

Whenever Josephine needed a bandage, Earle had to put it on her hands for her, using cotton gauze pads held on with adhesive tape. In those days, dressings were so fiddly that it was almost impossible to put bandages on your own hands.

Dressings came in the form of big cotton gauze pads.

You taped the pad over the cut or burn using medical tape.

As Josephine used her hands a lot, the dressings soon fell off.

Josephine needed a way to patch up her fingers herself, while Earle was at work. So he invented a special bandage just for her.

Handy bandages

Earle's idea was simple. He cut small squares of gauze bandage, and stuck them along a strip of medical tape. Then he stuck a length of crinoline (a kind of stiff fabric) on top, and rolled the tape up. All Josephine had to do was cut a piece off, peel off the crinoline and wrap the sticky strip around her finger.

This should do it!

Mini squares of gauze bandage   Strip of tape   Crinoline backing strip

Into production

Earle told his bosses, the Johnson brothers, about his invention. When he showed them how he could put a dressing on his own hand, they were impressed. They started manufacturing the bandages that same year, 1920, using the name BAND-AID®.

At first, BAND-AID® adhesive bandages were made by hand, just like Earle's own version. They came in a strip 7cm (3in) wide by 45cm (18in) long. Unfortunately, they didn't sell well. But in 1924, the company found a way to make smaller adhesive bandages using an automatic machine. The new version was much more popular, and adhesive bandages soon became widespread.

A 1921 package of BAND-AID® bandages

String opener

In 1940, Johnson & Johnson began making BAND-AIDs® in wrappers with a tiny red string inside. You pulled the string to open the wrapper. These "tear strings" are now used on many other products too, such as bags of pet food and food packages.

Worldwide and beyond

Since 1920, we've used billions and billions of small, light, convenient adhesive bandages. They've replaced bandages in most homes, soldiers carry them into war zones, and astronauts take them into space.

As for Earle Dickson, he was rewarded for his idea by being made Vice-President of Johnson & Johnson – a job he kept all his life.

Decorated bandages were introduced in 1956. Modern designs include cartoon characters and animal prints.

Seeing our insides

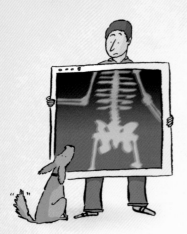

X-rays can show you your skeleton because they pass easily through soft, light tissue such as your organs – but not through hard, heavy objects like your bones. Where the rays get blocked, an image of your bones shows up.

Before x-rays were invented, no one thought it was possible to see through the human body. So when the mysterious rays were first used, many people thought they were magic.

Mystery rays

In 1895, a German scientist, Wilhelm Roentgen, was experimenting with a cathode ray tube – a kind of glass tube with the air sucked out of it. When an electric current is passed through a gas in the tube, it creates a "cathode ray" – a stream of tiny particles called electrons.

Scientists often tested their cathode ray tubes using a special screen covered with chemicals that glowed when a cathode ray hit them. But they knew cathode rays could only travel a short distance. Roentgen found that his screen glowed even when it was at the other end of a desk from the tube. Weirdest of all, when he put his hand up to the screen, he saw an image of his bones.

X-ray science

At first, Roentgen didn't know what his mystery rays were made of. But experiments later showed that they were a type of electromagnetic wave, like light and radio waves.

Radio waves are very long electromagnetic waves.

Light waves are medium-length electromagnetic waves that our eyes can detect.

X-rays are very short electromagnetic waves. They are invisible and can pass through most substances.

Oooooh!

Cathode ray tube

Roentgen realized that, besides cathode rays, the tube must be making some other kind of rays that could pass through solid objects. He had no idea what they were, so he called them "x-rays."

X-ray photos

Next, Roentgen found out how to make x-ray photos by firing the rays at photographic paper. He made an x-ray of his wife Bertha's hand and sent it to some scientist friends. Soon, x-rays took the world by storm.

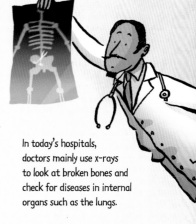

In today's hospitals, doctors mainly use x-rays to look at broken bones and check for diseases in internal organs such as the lungs.

Doctors used x-rays to look inside wounded soldiers.

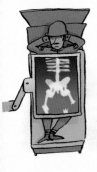

Dentists used them to examine rotten teeth.

Some companies even advertized x-ray-proof underwear!

Ultrasound scanning is often used to look at babies before they are born, as it is safer for them than an x-ray.

Risky rays

At first, people thought x-rays were safe. Scientists and doctors often used their hands to test the ray. But when people started to die of cancer after too many x-rays, scientists realized that they could be harmful. Doctors today still use x-rays to look inside people's bodies, but modern x-rays are much weaker and not so dangerous.

A patient in an MRI scanner

Beyond x-rays

Since Roentgen discovered x-rays, many more methods of looking inside our bodies have been invented. They include MRI (magnetic resonance imaging) which uses strong radio waves, and ultrasound scanning, which bounces sound off your insides to make a picture.

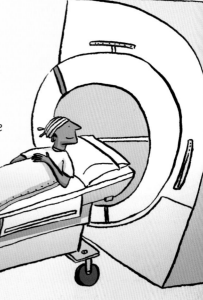

Paper pioneers

Today, paper is everywhere – in books, magazines, junk mail and sticky notes. But thousands of years ago, no one had any. So where did paper come from?

Before paper

Before paper was invented, some people, such as the Sumerians, wrote on clay tablets.

Papyrus grows in shallow water and swamps along the banks of the River Nile.

Writing was invented long before paper, so people needed something to write on. Some wrote on soft clay with a stick, and waited for it to dry. Others wrote on slate or wood. But all these were horribly heavy.

The ancient Indians wrote on leaves. Leaves were lighter, but they rotted away. And the ancient Chinese used silk, but it was fragile and expensive.

Papyrus

Then, about 5,000 years ago, the ancient Egyptians tried something new, using the stems of a river plant called papyrus to create flat sheets.

They had invented an early kind of paper. (In fact our word "paper" comes from the word papyrus.) Papyrus was great for writing on – but it took a long time to make, so it was too expensive for anyone but the rich.

1. First, the Egyptians peeled the pithy papyrus stems and sliced them into strips.

2. They arranged the strips in layers to make a flat sheet. The naturally sticky papyrus strips glued themselves together.

3. The papyrus sheet was polished smooth with a stone.

4. Finally, several sheets were stuck together to make a scroll.

A new recipe

As with many other inventions, the Chinese were the first to invent proper paper. The ancient Chinese liked writing things down – history, lists, laws, poems and stories. In about the year 100, a court official, Ts'ai Lun, tried making something cheaper than silk to write on. He mashed tree bark, hemp plants and cotton rags together in water, strained the pulp through a cloth, and pressed it into a flat sheet. After drying out in the sun, it was light, smooth, and perfect for writing on.

Ts'ai Lun had made the first modern paper. It was cheap, and it caught on. By 1400, people all over Asia and Europe were making paper from rags and mashed plants.

Ts'ai Lun's recipe of hemp, rags and bark made his paper light but strong.

Wasp-watching

Soon, so many books were being made that paper-makers began to run out of rags.

Then, in 1719, French scientist René Réaumur noticed some wasps chewing up wood to make their papery nests. He saw that paper could be made from solid wood.

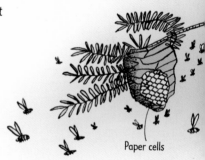

Paper cells

Wasps use their jaws to scrape wood shavings from trees. They mix the wood with their saliva (spit) and chew it into a pulp, then use it to build their nest cells and walls. As the pulp dries, it hardens into a kind of light, strong paper.

Big business

The paper-makers tried Réaumur's idea of making paper from wood pulp, and it worked. Today, most paper still comes from wood. It's made in huge factories by giant paper-making machines. And we use more of it than ever.

Around the year 1400, Chinese paper makers began using another ingredient in their paper – old, unwanted books. They had invented paper recycling. We now recycle more and more used paper, as this reduces the number of trees that have to be chopped down to make new paper.

When paper is recycled, it is mixed with water until it is a soggy mush.

The mush is sprayed out onto a moving wire screen

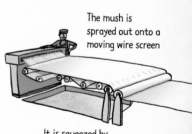

It is squeezed by rollers, dried and wound into a big roll.

> This book's much too long!

Books with pages
Books didn't always have pages. Long ago, books were written on long scrolls and rolled up. But starting in about the year 300, people began folding up scrolls. This led to the idea of tying pages together to make a book.

Block-printed books often had lots of pictures, because they were easier to carve than words.

Early Chinese type blocks contained one Chinese character on each block.

Books for everyone

In medieval times, books weren't something everyone could own. They were rare and very expensive, because they took a very long time to make. So when Johann Gutenberg invented a new, quicker and easier way to print books, he changed people's lives.

Handmade books

Before printing presses, most books were copied out, one at a time, by hand. At first, in Europe, monks in monastery libraries did most of this laborious handwriting. From about 1200, professional handwriters called scribes did the job too.

There was also a type of simple printing called block printing. You carved a page of text and illustrations onto a block of wood, inked it and pressed it onto the paper. But this still took a very, very long time.

Moveable type

In around 1045, a Chinese man, Bi Sheng, came up with a really clever invention: moveable type. Instead of carving whole pages of words, he made individual carved clay blocks that he could rearrange to make different pages of text. The trouble was, instead of an alphabet, Chinese writing used thousands of symbols, called characters. There was a different one for each word. This made Bi's system difficult to use, since there had to be thousands of different kinds of printing blocks. But the idea of moveable type itself was brilliant. In Europe, the same idea would revolutionize printing.

70

Gutenberg gets it right

In the 1430s, Johann Gutenberg, a jeweler in Strasburg, Germany, began behaving oddly. He kept borrowing money from his friends and disappearing into his workshop for days. What they didn't know was that he was secretly working on a new printing method.

Although he probably hadn't heard of Bi Sheng, he had had a similar idea – making separate pieces of type for all the letters of the alphabet. He also designed a printing press, with a frame to hold all the letters arranged into pages, ready for printing.

Eventually, someone sued Gutenberg for not paying back some money he'd borrowed. He didn't have the cash, so he had to hand over all his printing equipment instead. The secret of his press came out, and the idea spread like wildfire. Soon, books were rolling off newly-built presses all over Europe.

Gutenberg developed a system for making lots of pieces of metal type quickly and easily.

Gutenberg's press was designed to work with movable type.

Paper presses down on top.

Tray of type arranged into a page and inked

Reading revolution

Gutenberg's press was one of the most important inventions ever. By rearranging the letters, printers could set up their presses to make a new book in just a few days – then print off thousands of copies.

Books became much cheaper and widely available, and more and more people learned to read. Now everyone could learn new things, read poems and stories and hear about new ideas.

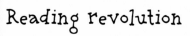

A modern offset printer is controlled by a computer.

Paper supply

Moving on
Nowadays, we rarely use moveable type. Other inventions such as offset printing and computerized digital laser printing have made book production even faster. But Gutenberg-style presses dominated the book industry for about 400 years, from 1450-1850.

Cut and printed sheets

The brilliant biro

Ballpoint pens are everywhere. Millions and millions and MILLIONS of them are sold every day, all over the world. And it's all thanks to one man. His name was Mr. Biró.

Who was Biró?

Laszlo Biró was a writer and artist in Hungary in the 1930s. He worked as a journalist, and was always having to scribble things down. But he hated messy, inky fountain pens! In those days, they were what most people used for writing. They had a steel nib and a kind of tiny tank, called a reservoir, which you filled up with ink. Unfortunately, this led to lots of blots and splotches.

On a visit to a printing factory, Biró saw that, unlike normal pen ink, printer's ink didn't smudge. He tried putting some printer's ink in his fountain pen, but it was so thick and gloopy that it clogged up the pen.

So Biró came up with another way to make the thick printer's ink flow, using a specially designed pen with a rolling ball in the tip. Instead of flowing freely from a nib, the sticky ink coated the ball, and the ball left a line of ink as it rolled across the paper. Here's how it worked:

A new idea?

Biró dreamed up the ballpoint himself, but it had been thought of before. US inventor John Loud had the idea for a kind of ballpoint pen in 1888, but he couldn't make it work. Biró didn't copy Loud's idea – he didn't even know about it.

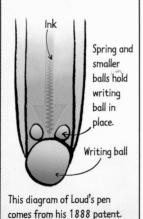

Ink

Spring and smaller balls hold writing ball in place.

Writing ball

This diagram of Loud's pen comes from his 1888 patent.

Biró fitted a ball bearing into the end of an ink-filled tube.

The gloopy ink flowed around the bearing, like lubricating grease.

Ink

Ball bearing

As the ball rolled, it drew a perfect, non-smudgy line.

Going overseas

Laszlo Biró's brother Georg helped him
with the design, and in 1938 the two
brothers patented their pen. But then the
Second World War broke out in Europe, and
Laszlo and Georg fled to Argentina. There,
they took out an Argentinian patent as well,
and kept working on the pen, designing new
versions that were easier to use and manufacture.

Dear Mother...

Ballpoints were great for
the air force. They didn't
need constant refills, and
they worked anywhere –
even at high altitudes.

Ballpoint breakthrough

In 1943, still in Argentina, Laszlo met a British army
officer named Henry Martin. Martin thought the
no-mess ballpoint was a great idea. He bought the
rights to manufacture ballpoint pens for the British air
force. They were so handy, reliable and easy to use
that word spread, and everyone started wanting to
buy them. By Christmas 1945, ballpoint pens were on
sale to the public in Britain, Argentina and the USA.
Even though the first models were quite expensive,
they were a huge hit. The new gadget sold by the
thousand.

The Bic® Cristal™ biro is a
design classic. There are billions
of them in the world today.

Biros for all

In the 1950s, French company Bic found a
way to make a super-cheap, mass-produced ballpoint
pen. Named the Bic® Cristal™, it took over the world.

    Today, thousands of companies make ballpoints with
many different names. But we still remember their
inventor with the word "biro" – the everyday name
for a ballpoint pen.

No sweat

Did you know it's also thanks
to Biró that we have roll-on
deodorant? The deodorant
company 'Mum' used the
rollerball idea from
Biró's invention
in 1952, to
create a new
way of applying
deodorant.

Don't forget to buy more sticky notes!

Non-sticky glue! Brilliant!

Sticky messages

Want to leave a message for your friend, write handy notes in a schoolbook, or remind yourself to record a TV show? A sticky note or "Post-it® note" is perfect for the job. It's one of the simplest and most useful of all 20th century inventions.

Non-sticky glue

In 1968, Dr. Spencer Silver was working for an American company, 3M, which made adhesive tapes and chemical coatings. He was trying to develop a new, extra-strong glue — but his experiments produced something quite different: a glue that wasn't very sticky at all. If you stuck something with it, it easily came apart.

Silver and his bosses knew the glue must be useful for something. But what? Silver thought of covering a noticeboard with it, so that notices could be stuck onto it and pulled off again. But the idea never took off.

Choir chaos

Fast-forward to 1974, when another 3M worker, Art Fry, was singing with his church choir. Fry needed to mark the right hymns in his hymn book each Sunday, so he'd put in scraps of paper as bookmarks. But they always fell out, leaving him scrabbling on the floor.

Sticky spheres

How does Spencer Silver's non-sticky glue work? It's made of a chemical that forms tiny spheres called "acrylate-copolymer microspheres" that are no bigger than the thickness of paper.

The spheres are actually very sticky, but only a small part of each sphere comes into contact with a flat surface, so the glue easily comes unstuck.

Microspheres

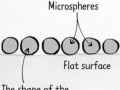

Flat surface

The shape of the microspheres makes them easy to unstick.

Oops! Not again...

"That glue would do!"

Then Art Fry remembered the non-sticky glue his colleague had come up with. He took some of the glue from work and tried pasting a bit along one edge of a piece of paper. Ta-daa! He had invented sticky bookmarks. They stuck to the page, but could easily be removed without tearing it.

A message for you

Back at work, Fry started developing his idea into a real company product. It took several years before the scientists at the company found a way to make the non-sticky glue hold permanently to the bookmark, while not sticking to the book.

One day, during his experiments, Fry wrote a note to a friend on one of his bookmarks. The friend wrote a reply on it, and stuck it back on his desk. Soon, lots of people who worked at 3M started doing the same. The sticky pieces of paper weren't just useful as bookmarks – they made great reminder notes, mini-messages and labels. 3M started manufacturing them, and launched them with the name "Post-it® notes" in 1980.

Sticky solutions

No one realized they needed sticky notes until they came along – but now, people can't manage without them. You can find them stuck all over most offices and other workplaces, and in millions of homes and schools too. In fact, trillions of sticky notes are stuck somewhere every year.

There is a strip of glue under the top edge of each note.

The notes come stuck together in a pad, ready to peel off.

The classic Post-it® design is a 3-inch (7.5cm) square in a pale canary yellow. One reason Post-it® notes work so well is that they stand out from their surroundings, making messages and reminders easy to spot.

New versions
Although 3M patented their Post-it® notes, sticky notes are now made by many other companies too. They come in dozens of shades and in fun shapes such as telephones and speech bubbles. There are even electronic versions that can make a virtual post-it note appear on your computer screen.

Brainy Braille

L ouis Braille went blind as a young child, but he couldn't resign himself to a life without books. So, while he was still a teenager, he came up with a brilliant invention...

Braille's boyhood

Besides being a brilliant student, Louis learned to play the cello and the organ. Music was something he could enjoy just as well as ever.

Braille was born in France in 1809. Aged three, playing in his father's workshop, he hurt his eye with an awl (a pointed tool). Both his eyes became infected, and he went blind. But Louis was very brainy, and he didn't want his disability to stop his education. He went to a local school with the other children, and then, when he turned 11, to a school for the blind in Paris.

Bulky books

The school's books for the blind used very large letters that stuck up from the page. Each book was very big and heavy.

The school for the blind that Louis went to had a few books with raised letters for the students to feel. But reading them was a nightmare. To make them easy to feel, the letters had to be huge, so reading them took ages. Louis knew there must be a better way.

Barbier's "night writing" used sticking-up dots to stand for different sounds.

Then, in 1821, an army captain named Charles Barbier visited the school. He'd developed a code of raised dots called "night writing" to allow his soldiers to swap messages in the dark. The soldiers found the code too awkward to use on missions. But Barbier wondered if the school for the blind might find it more useful. Louis was thrilled when he first felt the code. It was very hard to use, but it gave him an idea. He decided to design his own, better version.

The symbols in Barbier's code were so big, you had to move your finger around to count the dots in each one.

Louis's letters

Louis realized that the reason Barbier's code was hard to read was that each clump of dots – or "cell" – was too big to feel with a single fingertip. So he designed a new cell with space for just 6 dots. Although the cell was smaller, Louis found enough different dot patterns to stand for every letter of the alphabet. So he could write normal words and sentences in his code. The writing could be read fast, with one finger. And as well as reading, blind people could now write, too – by pressing dots into the paper themselves.

With a maximum of six dots, Braille's letters could be recognized at once. You could read just by running your finger along the lines of writing.

Changing the world

The first Braille book was published in 1827, when Louis was 18. But at first the code didn't catch on. It was only after Braille died that people finally saw how useful it could be. Now, Braille is used all over the world. As well as reading books, it helps blind people to use computers and the Internet.

The basic Braille alphabet

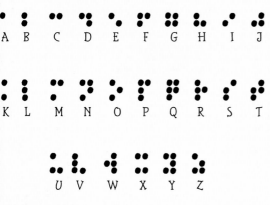

A B C D E F G H I J

K L M N O P Q R S T

U V W X Y Z

After Braille?

Many blind people use Braille display machines, which link to computers and turn a page of text into a series of pins that can be touched as they pop up. After a line has been read, the user can 'refresh' the display in order to read additional lines. But there is now new technology that turns text into speech, and some blind children use this instead of learning Braille. So Braille could gradually become a thing of the past.

Pop-up pins

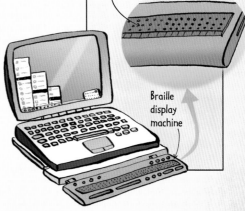

Braille display machine

WRITING TOOLS
THROUGH THE AGES

Writing is incredibly useful – it allows us to store facts, make lists and send messages. And we've been doing it for more than 5,000 years.

3200 BC Clay tablets

Cuneiform, the first known writing, developed in the ancient middle-eastern civilization of Sumeria more than 5,000 years ago. It was written by pressing a wedge-shaped reed into wet clay to make little pictures.

By combining several pictures, you could express more complex ideas.

Grain   Plow   Harvest

2500 BC Brush and ink

Over 4,000 years ago people in Egypt and China were writing with simple pens and brushes dipped in ink. The first ink was made of soot mixed with water.

600 Quill pen

Quill pens, made from a bird's feather cut at an angle, date from about the year 600. They were invented in Spain and eventually became popular across Europe.

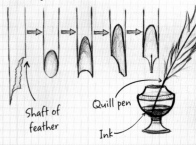

Shaft of feather

Quill pen

Ink

1300 BC Stylus and wax

Wax-covered wooden board

Stylus

Starting about 3,300 years ago, the Romans used a sharp tool called a stylus to scratch letters onto a wooden board covered with a layer of wax.

1500s Pencil

Pencils were invented in the early 1500s, after a graphite mine was discovered in England and people found that graphite was great for making marks. They made pencils by inserting a stick of graphite into a wooden holder.

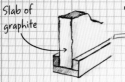

Slab of graphite

A piece of wood was cut with a square groove. A slab of graphite was slotted into the groove.

The graphite was broken off level with the top of the groove. A thin slat of wood was glued to the top, leaving the graphite encased.

To make a smoother pencil, the wood could then be sanded and shaped.

1803 Metal nib

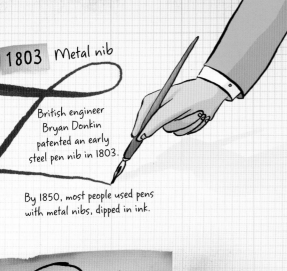

British engineer Bryan Donkin patented an early steel pen nib in 1803.

By 1850, most people used pens with metal nibs, dipped in ink.

1868 Typewriter

In 1868 a new way of writing came along when news editor Christopher Latham Sholes, working with a team of friends, invented the typewriter.

1884 Fountain pen

Even with typewriters, people still needed pens. In 1884 Lewis Edson Waterman invented the fountain pen, which carried its own supply of ink.

1938 Ballpoint pen

Laszlo Biró patented the first working ballpoint pen, or biro, in 1938 (see page 72 for his story).

1978 Word processor

As computers developed, electric and computerized typewriters were built. Around 1978, typewriters began to be replaced by word-processing software that could be used with a computer to write letters, novels, or anything else.

Word-processing software lets you make changes and correct mistakes as you write, before printing out your document.

1962 Felt-tip pen

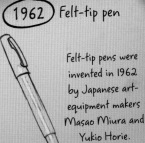

Felt-tip pens were invented in 1962 by Japanese art-equipment makers Masao Miura and Yukio Horie.

One can allow divers to breathe by lowering a bronze tank into the water.

The ancient Greek scientist Aristotle described how a heavy metal or pottery jar or tank could be lowered into the water upside-down to trap a supply of air.

A diver could breathe the air by standing up inside the jar.

The jar had to stay this way up!

Going under...

There are all kinds of reasons to go underwater — to watch wildlife, catch fish or collect sunken treasure. But humans can't breathe underwater — so inventors have had to invent diving suits.

Air pockets

Since ancient times, people have used pots and barrels to make simple diving bells that can store air underwater. The ancient Greek scientist Aristotle described this more than 2,300 years ago. The trouble was, the oxygen in the air was soon used up, so dives couldn't last long.

Breathing tubes

People soon thought of connecting the diver's mouth to the surface with a breathing tube — but these only work in very shallow water. In deep water, water pressure squeezes your chest and it's hard to breathe air in.

In 1650, Otto Von Geuricke invented the air pump to help him create vacuums for his experiments. In 1837, German inventor Augustus Siebe used this technology to design the first true diving suit. It used an air pump to force air down the tube, helping the diver to breathe in.

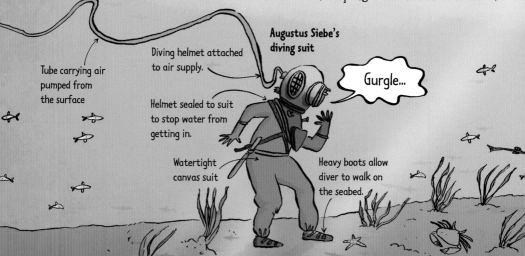

Tube carrying air pumped from the surface

Diving helmet attached to air supply.

Augustus Siebe's diving suit

Helmet sealed to suit to stop water from getting in.

Watertight canvas suit

Gurgle...

Heavy boots allow diver to walk on the seabed.

Floating free

Suits like Siebe's were used for over a century, but they weren't ideal. Early materials were heavy, and divers had to trudge along slowly. And, as the suit was linked to the surface, the diver couldn't move around freely.

The answer, of course, was to take an air supply with you. In 1865, French inventors Benoît Rouquayrol and Auguste Denayrouze were the first to try this, using a tank of compressed air attached to the diver's back.

SCUBA suits

Many inventors now began to experiment with tanks of compressed air or oxygen. This became known as SCUBA gear – Self-Contained Underwater Breathing Apparatus. But there was a problem. As the tanks released air under high pressure, some divers died from breathing in too much oxygen too fast.

The amazing aqualung

The solution came in 1943, thanks to French underwater pioneer Jacques Cousteau, and his friend Emile Gagnan. They designed a special valve to let air out of the tank at the same pressure as the surrounding water, to make breathing easy and safe. They called the new diving gear the "aqualung."

At last, divers could explore safely. Cousteau later described the fantastic feeling of freedom as he tested the aqualung for the first time...

Glug...

Rouquayrol and Denayrouze's suit did have an air supply tube, but it could be disconnected to allow the diver a few minutes of freedom.

I kicked the fins languidly and traveled down, gaining speed, watching the beach rolling past. I stopped kicking and the momentum carried me on a fabulous glide...

The quiet-loud machine

If you study music, you'll probably learn the piano - the best-known, most-played instrument of all. But did you know it's a far more recent invention than most other instruments?

PLUNK!

A few hundred years ago, although there were plenty of keyboard intruments, you might think they sounded as if they were being played by robots (except that robots hadn't been invented). However hard you pressed a key, the sound came out the same – PLUNK!

The typical keyboard instrument was the harpsichord, which looked like a piano, but contained quills and wire strings. When you pressed a key, a quill plucked a string, always the same way and always at the same volume – so there wasn't much variation in the sound.

Plink!

There was another instrument, the clavichord, which did have volume control. When you pressed a clavichord key, a piece of metal hit a string. Pressing harder made the note louder. But, overall, the clavichord was very quiet. It could barely fill a small room with sound, so it was useless for concerts.

Can't hear a thing!

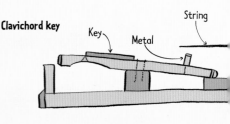

Clavichord key

Key

Metal

String

82

It must be quiet one moment... loud the next.

"We're waiting!"

Keyboard composers were fed up with writing endless trills and twiddly parts in their harpsichord music to make it more interesting. What they really wanted was a keyboard that could express emotions, like a violin.

Cunning Cristofori

In 1698, Italian harpsichord-maker Bartolomeo Cristofori decided to crack the problem of the clunky keyboard. He made a "gravicembalo col piano e forte" – a "harpsichord with quiet and loud." By 1709, he'd built three. Here's how he did it.

Composers during the 17th century were fed up with harpsichords. They wanted something new.

Pianoforte key

A clever mechanism made the hammer move much faster than the key. Pressing the key hard made a very loud sound.

Instead of plucking a quill, each key made a hammer hit the strings.

String

Hammer

But a gentle touch made the hammer hit the string softly.

Key

The instrument made a rich, ringing sound, loud or soft, depending on how hard you hit the keys. Soon, composers were all writing for the amazing new "pianoforte," or piano.

From grand to electronic

Piano-makers experimented with different designs, including the upright piano. It allowed people to have a piano in a normal-sized home. Today, we also have touch-sensitive electronic keyboards that can mimic the sound of a real piano.

Naming the piano

Cristofori's name for his invention, "gravicembalo col piano e forte," was shortened to "pianoforte" meaning "quiet-loud." This was shortened even more to "piano" – meaning "quiet."

Cristofori's first pianos were large and long, a design now known as a grand piano.

83

Taking photos

For centuries, people longed to be able to capture real-life scenes directly onto paper. Now, thanks to the invention of the camera, we can.

The "camera obscura"

The first type of camera was the "camera obscura," Latin for "dark room." It was a dark chamber with a tiny hole in one wall to let in light. An upside-down image appeared on the wall opposite the hole. The Arabic scientist and inventor Alhazen made an early "camera obscura" in around 1020 – nearly 1,000 years ago.

How it works

Light rays travel in straight lines. When light reflected from an object passes through a narrow hole, the rays switch to form a reversed image.

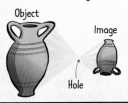

Object

Image

Hole

Alhazen came from Basra, in what is now Iraq, but spent many years in Egypt. He made many discoveries about light, lenses and vision.

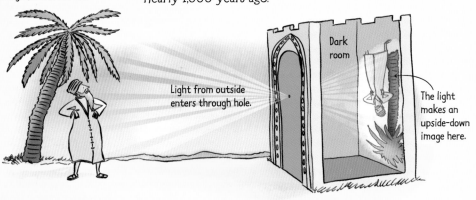

Light from outside enters through hole.

Dark room

The light makes an upside-down image here.

Picture boxes

Beginning in the 1500s, many artists used small "camera obscura" boxes to help them sketch accurately. The box collected an image from outside and focused it onto a glass screen so that it could be traced. But although they could copy them, the artists couldn't keep the pictures or print them out on paper. They were made of light, and only existed inside the camera.

A 16th-century artist using a box "camera obscura." Artists placed a piece of paper on the glass screen and traced the image.

Glass screen

A lens helped to focus the light rays clearly.

Mirror

The first photograph

Over time, scientists found that some chemicals changed color when light shone on them. In 1826, French scientist Joseph Niépce put a sheet of metal coated with a chemical called bitumen inside a "camera obscura." He pointed it out of a window for eight hours. The light shining on the bitumen left a permanent image – the first ever photo.

The image Niépce made, showing buildings, rooftops and a tree, was the first ever true photograph.

Faster photos

Niépce's invention was brilliant, but not very useful. It took eight hours to take a photo! So, through the 1830s, inventors tested ways to make photography faster.

Frenchman Louis Daguerre found a way to make images on chemical-coated sheets of copper. His photos, known as Daguerreotypes, took half an hour to take. Meanwhile, English inventor William Fox Talbot used chemical-covered paper instead. It worked in minutes, and each photo could be printed again and again.

Can you hold that for 30 minutes?

People had to sit still for half an hour for a Daguerreotype portrait.

Talbot's paper created a "negative" image. This could be used to make lots of copies.

Photos for everyone

By the 1850s, anyone could have their photo taken in a photo studio. And in 1888 US businessman George Eastman launched the Kodak No. 1, the first camera for people to use at home. Today, with digital cameras and camera phones, almost everyone has a camera, and millions of moments in time are captured every day.

Kodak No. 1

EVERYDAY INVENTIONS

There's space in this book for just a few more inventions – a selection of the everyday objects, gadgets and tools we can hardly imagine life without.

6400 BC   Mirror

Early mirrors were made from obsidian, a type of natural glass from volcanoes, cut and polished smooth.

The mirror is one of the oldest everyday inventions – it dates from more than 8,000 years ago. The first known mirrors were found in the ruins of Catal Huyuk, a stone-age settlement in what is now Turkey.

600 BC   Coins

The first coins were made about 2,600 years ago in Lydia, also in present-day Turkey. People collected electrum (a mixture of silver and gold) from the River Pactolus, and made it into bean-shaped lumps to use as money.

Lydian coins

Soon, people started stamping coins with pictures to show what they were worth – creating flattened coin shapes.

2000 BC   Lock and key

The door lock was invented in ancient Egypt about 4,000 years ago.

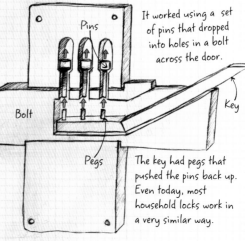

It worked using a set of pins that dropped into holes in a bolt across the door.

Pins

Bolt

Key

Pegs

The key had pegs that pushed the pins back up. Even today, most household locks work in a very similar way.

1498   Toothbrush

The Chinese invented the bristle toothbrush in 1498. The first ones were made from pig bristles attached to a piece of bone or bamboo.

Pig bristles

Bone

1938

Nylon bristle toothbrushes, which we use today, were first made in 1938.

1837 Postage stamp

Before postage stamps, you had to calculate the cost of mailing each letter according to how much it weighed and how far it went. In 1837 an English schoolteacher, Rowland Hill, came up with the idea of pre-paid postage stamps, with a simple flat rate of one penny per letter.

The world's first postage stamp, the Penny Black, came out in 1840 and was an instant success.

1893 Toaster

Electric toasters were invented in 1893, but they often burned the toast. So US inventor Charles Strite invented a toaster that popped the toast up when it was done. At first it was just for hotels and cafés. A smaller model designed for toasting at home was released in 1926.

A 1920s early pop-up toaster

1899 Paperclip

A Norwegian, Johan Vaaler, took out the first paperclip patent in 1899.

Vaaler's first paperclip design

Vaaler's design was a simple wire rectangle, with the wire overlapping on one side.

The paperclips we use today are based on an oval-shaped version, developed by a company called Gem at around the same time.

The "Gem" paperclip

1952 Barcode

There's a barcode on almost everything you buy, containing the product details and price as a code of black and white stripes that can be read by a special scanner.

Two students, Bernard Silver and Norman Woodland, invented the barcode in 1952. Their first design was circle-shaped, like a bullseye.

After years of improvements, barcodes were first used in stores in 1966. Rectangular barcodes became widespread in the 1970s.

1964 The first computer mouse

US inventor Dr. Douglas Engelbart thought up the computer mouse in 1964. The first version was made of wood, had one button and could do basic pointing and clicking on a screen. Engelbart named it "an X-Y position indicator for a display system" – but later called it the "mouse" because its wire looked like a tail.

The two wheels allowed the mouse to move up and down (Y axis) and from left to right (X axis).

Button

X-axis wheel

Y-axis wheel

Wire

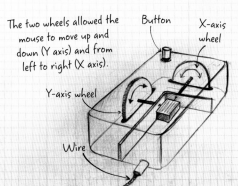

A modern barcode

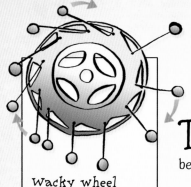

Wacky wheel

The overbalanced wheel is a classic perpetual motion design. As the wheel turns, the weighted levers tip over, pulling it down on one side. However, the weight of the levers is always the same on both sides of the wheel, so it can't work.

Crazy ideas?

These inventions seemed like a great idea at the time, but failed to get off the ground. But one day, they could still be a huge success...

Perpetual motion machine

Beginning in the 700s, inventors have been trying to build a perpetual motion machine – a machine that can keep moving forever without an energy source. No one has ever made this idea work, but scientists are still working on new versions. If they do develop a successful design, it will change the laws of science, and solve the world's energy problems.

One idea for a perpetual motion machine was a windmill that powered a giant set of bellows to blow its own sails around.

Self-cleaning house

US inventor Frances Gabe began building her own self-cleaning house in the 1950s – and still lives in it. The house has sprinklers that spray each room with soapy water. The furniture is waterproof and there are covers to protect valuable items. The wardrobe washes clothes, the cupboards wash the dishes and the bookshelves dust themselves.

Gabe's invention never became popular. But, new inventions such as robotic vacuum cleaners and dirt-repelling glass could soon make self-cleaning houses the norm.

Gabe, who worked as a builder, designed her house because she hated housework.

Sticky foam gun

Police forces and armies
around the world are trying to
develop non-lethal weapons that
can stop criminals in their tracks without
harming them. One idea, developed in the early 1990s,
was a sticky foam spray that could glue enemies to the spot.
But, once they were stuck, they couldn't be
arrested or removed until a clean-up team arrived.
And if the foam hit someone's face, it could stop
them from breathing, so it wasn't that safe after all.

    Now, inventors have found new uses for sticky foam,
such as guarding hi-security doors. If intruders try to break
in, the foam bursts out, trapping them. Meanwhile, inventors
are working on new non-leathal weapons, including blasts
of low-frequency sound that make people feel ill and dizzy.

Sticky foam was originally
designed to be sprayed from a
gun onto escaping criminals.

Very low, deep sounds can
affect the brain and other
organs, making people feel
dizzy and sick.

A ladder to space

In the Bible, Jacob dreams of a ladder to Heaven for the
angels to use. And in 1895, Russian scientist Konstantin
Tsiolkovsky saw the Eiffel Tower, and dreamed of a tower
that would reach space. Unfortunately, no tower this high
could support its own weight. In the 1950s and 1960s,
scientists developed a new idea — a cable linking the
Earth to a satellite in orbit. But there was still no material
strong enough to make it a reality.

    In the 1990s, however, NASA began work on a new
design for a space cable made of super-strong carbon
nanotube fibers. There are problems to
solve, but the "space elevator" is now a
serious plan. It could make going into space
much cheaper and easier than it is now.

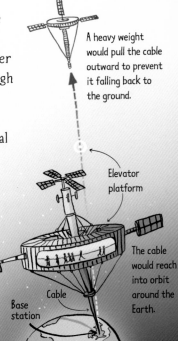

A heavy weight
would pull the cable
outward to prevent
it falling back to
the ground.

Elevator
platform

The cable
would reach
into orbit
around the
Earth.

Cable

Base
station

Inventions timeline

Few inventions can be pinned down to a single date, or even a single inventor. So this timeline shows approximate dates when inventions appeared (using the symbol 'c.'), and the main inventors behind them.

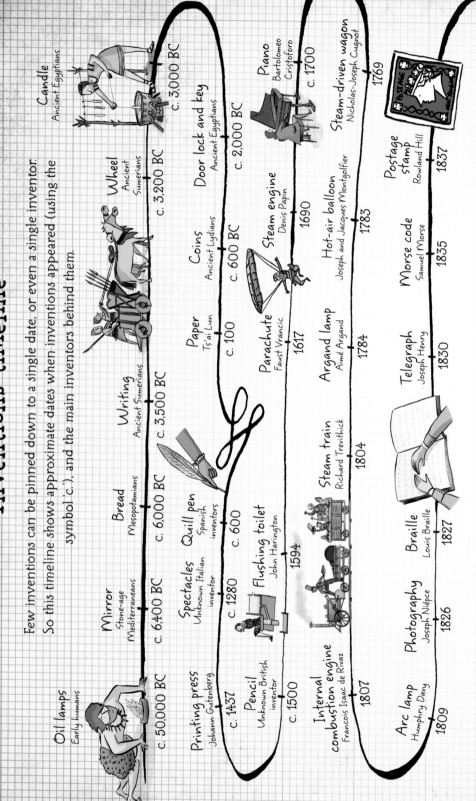

Oil lamps
Early humans
c. 50,000 BC

Mirror
Stone-age Mediterraneans
c. 6,400 BC

Bread
Mesopotamians
c. 6,000 BC

Writing
Ancient Sumerians
c. 3,500 BC

Wheel
Ancient Sumerians
c. 3,200 BC

Candle
Ancient Egyptians
c. 3,000 BC

Door lock and key
Ancient Egyptians
c. 2,000 BC

Coins
Ancient Lydians
c. 600 BC

Paper
Ts'ai Lun
c. 100

Spectacles
Unknown Italian inventor
c. 1280

Quill pen
Spanish inventors
c. 600

Flushing toilet
John Harington
1594

Parachute
Faust Vrancic
1617

Steam engine
Denis Papin
1690

Piano
Bartolomeo Cristofori
c. 1700

Printing press
Johann Gutenberg
c. 1437

Pencil
Unknown British inventor
c. 1500

Internal combustion engine
Francois Isaac de Rivaz
1807

Steam train
Richard Trevithick
1804

Argand lamp
Aimé Argand
1784

Hot-air balloon
Joseph and Jacques Montgolfier
1783

Steam-driven wagon
Nicholas-Joseph Cugnot
1769

Arc lamp
Humphry Davy
1809

Photography
Joseph Niépce
1826

Braille
Louis Braille
1827

Telegraph
Joseph Henry
1830

Morse code
Samuel Morse
1835

Postage stamp
Rowland Hill
1837

Airship
Henri
Giffard
1852

Chocolate
bar
Francis Fry
1847

Anaesthetic
Humphry Davy, Horace Wells
1840s

Kirkpatrick
Macmillan
1839

Diving suit
Augustus Siebe
1837

Fountain pen
Lewis Edson
Waterman
1884

Computer
Charles Babbage, John
Mauchly, J. Presper Eckert
1840-1946

Phonograph
Thomas Edison
1877

Telephone
Alexander
Graham Bell
1876

Jeans
Jacob Davis and
Levi Strauss
1873

Chewing gum
Thomas Adams
1869

Dishwasher
Josephine Garis
Cochran
1886

X-rays
Wilhelm Roentgen
1895

Radio
Guglielmo Marconi
c. 1900

Bubble gum
Walter Diemer
1928

Tape recording
Fritz Pfleumer
1928

Jet engine
Frank Whittle,
Hans von Ohain
1930

Domestic
pop-up toaster
Charles Strite
1926

Catseye
Percy Shaw
1933

Helicopter
Heinrich Focke
1936

Text message
Sent by Neil
Papworth to Richard
Jarvis on the
Vodafone network
1992

Post-it
note
Art Fry
1974

Internet
USA Defense
Advanced Research
Projects Agency
(DARPA)
1969

Biro
Laszlo Biró
1938

Compact
disc
James Russell
1965

Lightbulb
Heinrich Göbel, Joseph
Swan, Thomas Edison
1854-1878

Chips
George Crum
1853

Typewriter
Christopher
Latham Sholes
1868

Vacuum cleaner
Hubert Cecil Booth
1901

Adhesive
bandages
Earle Dickson
1920

Zipper
Gideon Sundback
1913

Velcro
Georges de Mestral
1941-1951

Computer
mouse
Douglas Engelbart
1964

LED
Scientists at Bell
Laboratories
1962

Plane
Orville and
Wilbur Wright
1903

Television
Boris Rosing, John
Logie Baird
1907-1925

Aqualung
Jacques Cousteau,
Emile Gagnan
1943

Felt-tip pen
Masao Miura,
Yukio Hori
1962

Microwave
oven
Percy Spencer
1945

Barcode
Bernard Silver and
Norman Woodland
1952

Cell phone
Scientists at Bell
Laboratories
1945

Self-cleaning
house
Frances Gabe
1950s

Glossary

anaesthetic A drug that numbs pain during surgery.

atoms Tiny particles that objects are made up of.

bacteria A type of tiny living thing.

biplane A plane with two sets of wings.

carbon fiber Fine thread or material made from carbon, or plastic reinforced with carbon thread.

carbonized Made into carbon by being burned.

carbon nanotubes Carbon molecules that form tiny, very strong tube shapes.

cathode ray tube A device that can make a picture appear on a screen by firing a beam of electrons at the screen along a tube.

circuit A loop made up of wires and other parts that can conduct electricity.

cog A wheel-shaped part with teeth around the outside, found inside many machines.

conduct If a material can conduct electricity, it means that electricity can flow through it.

current A flow of electricity through a wire or other object.

Dark Ages A name used for the time between 500 and 1000 in Europe. Also used to mean any time lacking in scientific study and progress.

dictation Speaking words so that they can be recorded.

digital Digital devices, such as computers, store information using numbers or symbols. This makes them different than "analog" devices such as vinyl records, which store information as a varying pattern.

electromagnetic spectrum (EMS) The full range of electromagnetic waves, from the shortest, Gamma rays, to the longest, radio waves.

electromagnetism A form of wave energy that includes light waves, radio waves, x-rays and microwaves.

electrons Very tiny particles found in atoms.

engineering Designing and building machines and systems to do useful jobs.

exhaust Waste gases given out by an engine.

filament A very thin strip of metal or another substance. The part of a light bulb that glows is a filament.

fluorescent Fluorescent substances glow when some types of electromagnetic energy hit them.

friction A force that makes two objects grip onto each other when rubbed together.

gasoline Fuel used to power cars, also called gas.

germs Tiny living things that can cause diseases in other things. Germs include some types of viruses and bacteria.

glider A winged flying machine that has no engine or other on-board power source.

hydrogen A type of gas that can be used as a fuel.

indentation A dent or small pit in a surface.

inert gases A group of gases, including neon and argon, that do not burn easily.

lens A curved piece of glass that bends light rays.

lever A stick-shaped part that rotates around a balancing point or pivot. Levers are an important part of many machines.

magnetron A device that emits microwaves.

materials Different kinds of substances.

medieval A word used to describe the time between about 500 and 1500.

microwaves A type of electromagnetic wave that can pass through food and heat it.

Middle Ages The period between about 500 and 1500, also known as medieval times.

military To do with the armed forces.

missile A bullet, bomb or other object that is thrown or fired at a target as a weapon.

modulation Changing a radio wave so that it contains a pattern that stores information.

molecule A small particle of a substance, made up of atoms joined together.

monoplane A plane with one set of wings.

non-lethal Designed not to cause death or serious injury.

orbit A circular path that an object follows around a larger object such as a planet. "To orbit" means to travel in an orbit.

oxygen A gas that humans and other animals need to breathe to stay alive.

patent An official license that protects an invention or idea from being copied or stolen. "To patent" something means to get a patent for it.

photovoltaic cell A device that takes in light and turns it into an electrical current.

piston A cylinder-shaped or disc-shaped part that moves to and fro inside a tube.

pollen Dust-like substance released by plants.

prehistoric A word for the time before historical records were written down.

program A set of instructions that tell a computer how to do a particular task.

propeller A device for moving a plane or boat forward, with angled blades that push against the air or water as the propeller spins around.

radar A system that can detect planes, clouds or other objects by beaming microwaves at them and collecting the patterns that bounce back.

radioactive A radioactive substance gives out particles or rays, such as gamma rays, which can be harmful.

radio waves A type of electromagnetic wave used to carry information over long distances.

Renaissance A period from about 1450 to 1700, when art, culture and science flourished in Europe.

satellite An object that travels around another object. Space satellites orbit around the Earth, passing on signals or making measurements.

scribe Someone whose job is to write by hand.

sewage Waste from sinks and toilets.

sewer A channel or tunnel that carries sewage.

silicon A substance found in sand and used to make parts of computers.

sterile Free from germs.

streamlined Shaped to move easily and smoothly through air or water.

termites Insects similar to ants.

ticker tape Narrow paper tape used to store information in the form of a series of dots.

transistor A device used in computers to allow them to do calculations.

Tropical To do with the tropics, the part of the Earth near the equator.

ultrasound Sound higher than humans can hear.

vacuum A completely empty space.

vacuum tube A type of tube with a vacuum inside, used in early computers.

vehicle A transportation device with wheels, such as a car.

vibrate To shake quickly back and forth.

wavelength The length of a wave, measured from one point on a wave to the same point on the next wave.

Index

Internet links

There are lots of websites with information about inventions, inventors and how things work. There are also fun activities you can try to see why some inventions just don't work at all. At the Usborne Quicklinks Website you'll find links to some great sites where you can find out more about hundreds of amazing inventors and inventions, see pictures and animations, look up all kinds of famous patents, and learn how to set up your own inventions and experiments.

For links to these sites, go to the Usborne Quicklinks Website at **www.usborne-quicklinks.com** and enter the keyword "inventions". When using the Internet, please follow the Internet safety guidelines shown on the Usborne Quicklinks Website. The links at Usborne Quicklinks are regularly reviewed and updated, but Usborne Publishing is not responsible for and does not accept liability for the content on any website other than its own. We recommend that children are supervised while using the Internet.

Every effort has been made to trace the copyright holders and correct tradename formats of the terms used in this book. If any terms have been used incorrectly, the publishers offer their sincere apologies and will rectify this in any subsequent editions following notification.

Art director: Mary Cartwright. Picture research by Ruth King. Additional editorial work by Alex Frith.